THE CENTRAL
MESSAGE
OF THE NEW
TESTAMENT

*Also by Joachim Jeremias
and published by SCM Press*

The Eucharistic Words of Jesus
Jerusalem in the Time of Jesus
New Testament Theology
The Parables of Jesus
The Prayers of Jesus
Rediscovering the Parables

JOACHIM JEREMIAS

The Central Message of the New Testament

SCM PRESS LTD

334 00156 0

First published 1965
by SCM Press Ltd
58 Bloomsbury Street, London WC1
Second impression 1981

Printed in Great Britain by
Richard Clay (The Chaucer Press) Ltd
Bungay, Suffolk

Contents

Preface

IT WAS a signal honour for me to be invited to deliver the four lectures which this little book contains as the Hewett Lectures of 1963, at Union Theological Seminary, New York; Episcopal Theological School, Cambridge; and Andover Newton Theological School. A lecture-tour in the United States, sponsored by the National Lutheran Council, gave me the additional privilege of lecturing to other theological faculties of various denominations. I shall never forget the simply overwhelming hospitality and kindness with which my wife and I were received in each place, and I wish to express my special thanks for the stimulation which I got from the discussions following the lectures.

JOACHIM JEREMIAS

ONE

Abba

1. God as 'Father' in the Old Testament

From earliest times, the Near East has been familiar
with the mythological idea that the deity is the father of
mankind or of certain human beings. Peoples, tribes, and
families picture themselves as being the offspring of a
divine ancestor. Particularly, it is the king, as represent-
ing his people, who enjoys a special share of the dig-
nity and power of a divine father. Whenever the word
'father' is used for a deity in this connection it implies
fatherhood in the sense of unconditional and irrevocable
authority.

All this is a mere commonplace in the history of religion.
But it is less well known that already very early the word
'father' as an epithet for the deity repeatedly carries a
specific overtone. In a famous Sumerian and Accadian

Note: The reader will find references to sources, discussion of the
literature, etc., in a more elaborate form of this first lecture which
is included in a collection of papers of mine ('Abba', *Untersuchungen
zur neutestamentlichen Theologie und Zeitgeschichte*, Göttingen, 1965).

hymn from Ur, the moon god Sin is invoked as 'Begetter, merciful in his disposing, who holds in his hand the life of the whole land'. And it is said of the Sumerian-Babylonian god Ea:

> *His wrath is like the deluge,*
> *his being reconciled like a merciful father.*

For orientals, the word 'father', as applied to God, thus encompasses, from earliest times, something of what the word 'mother' signifies among us.

This is even truer of the Old Testament. God is seldom spoken of as 'father', in fact only fourteen times. However, all of these occurrences are important. First of all, God when called 'father' is honoured as the Creator:

> *Is not he your father, who created you,*
> *who made you and established you?*
>
> (Deut. 32.6)

> *Have we not all one father?*
> *Has not one God created us?*
>
> (Mal. 2.10)

As the Creator, God is the Lord. He can expect to be honoured by obedience.

On the other hand, being a father, God is also thought of as merciful:

> *As a father pities his children,*
>   *so the Lord pities those who fear him.*
> *For he knows our frame;*
>   *he remembers that we are dust.*
>
> (Ps. 103.13f.)

Just because God is the Creator, he is full of fatherly indulgence for the weakness of his children.

It is quite obvious that in all these references the Old Testament reflects the ancient oriental concept of divine fatherhood. Still there are fundamental differences. The fact that in the Old Testament God is not the ancestor or progenitor, but the Creator, is not the least of them. Even more important is the fact that in the Old Testament divine fatherhood is related to Israel alone in a quite unparalleled manner. Israel has a particular relationship to God. Israel is God's first-born, chosen out of all peoples (Deut. 14.1f.). Moreover this election of Israel as God's first-born son was thought of as being rooted in a concrete historical action, the Exodus from Egypt. Combining God's fatherhood with a historical action involves a profound revision of the concept of God as Father. The certainty that God is Father and Israel his son is grounded not in mythology but in a unique act of salvation by God, which Israel had experienced in history.

However, it was not until the prophets that the concept of God as Father gained its full significance in the Old Testament. Again and again, the prophets are obliged to say that Israel repays God's fatherly love with constant ingratitude. Most of the prophetic statements about God as Father passionately and emphatically point to the contradiction that manifests itself between Israel's sonship and his godlessness.

> *Have you not just now called to me,*
> *' My father, thou art the friend of my youth –*
> *will he be angry for ever,*
>   *will he be indignant to the end?'*
> *Behold, you have spoken,*
>   *but you have done all the evil that you could.*
>   (Jer. 3.4f.)

> *I thought how I would set you among my sons,*
>   *and give you a pleasant land,*
> *a heritage most beauteous of all nations.*
> *And I thought you would call me, My Father,*
>   *and would not turn from following me.*
> *Surely, as a faithless wife leaves her husband,*
>   *so have you been faithless to me, O house of Israel.*
>   (Jer. 3.19f.)

> *A son honours his father,*
>   *and a servant his master.*
> *If then I am a father, where is my honour?*
>   *and if I am a master, where is my fear?*
>   (Mal. 1.6)

Israel's constant answer to this call to repentance is the cry: 'Thou art my (or: our) Father'—*abhinu atta*. In Third Isaiah, this cry is elaborated into a final appeal for God's mercy and forgiveness:

Look down from heaven and see,
  from thy holy and glorious habitation.
Where are thy zeal and thy might?
  The yearning of thy heart and thy compassion?
Do not withhold from me,
  for thou art our Father (abhinu atta),
though Abraham does not know us
  and Israel does not acknowledge us;
thou, O Lord, art our Father (abhinu atta)
  Our Redeemer from of old is thy name.
                    (Isa. 63.15f.)

Yet, O Lord, thou art our Father;
  we are the clay, and thou art our potter;
  we are all the work of thy hand.
Be not exceedingly angry, O Lord,
  and remember not iniquity for ever.
                    (Isa. 64.8f.)

God answers this appeal of Israel with forgiveness.
Hos. 11.1–11 draws a touching picture of this. God is
compared to a father who taught his little son Ephraim to
walk and carried him in his arms:

Yet it was I who taught Ephraim to walk,
  I took them up in my arms . . .
How can I give you up, O Ephraim!
  How can I hand you over, O Israel!
                    (Hos. 11.3, 8)

Similarly, the prophet Jeremiah has found the most
moving expressions for God's forgiveness:

With weeping they shall come,
and with consolations I will lead them back,
I will make them walk by brooks of water,
in a straight path in which they shall not stumble;
for I am a father to Israel,
and Ephraim is my first-born.

(Jer. 31.9)

God's fatherly mercy exceeds all human comprehension:

Is Ephraim my dear son?
Is he my darling child? . . .
Therefore my heart yearns for him;
I must have mercy on him, says the Lord.

(Jer. 31.20)

This is the final word of the Old Testament with regard to divine fatherhood: the 'must' of God's incomprehensible mercy and forgiveness.

2. Palestinian Judaism

Like the Old Testament, Palestinian Judaism in the time before Jesus was very reluctant to speak of God as Father. In the whole of the Qumran literature, for instance, which must have been composed before AD 68, there is just one single passage to be found where the name of father is applied to God.[1] Rabbinical Judaism used the epithet somewhat more freely, though not abundantly.

[1] 1QH 9.35f.

If we inquire what Jesus' Jewish contemporaries meant to express by giving God the name of father two characteristics emerge.

First, no one who is familiar with Judaism at this period will be astonished to find that the obligation to obey the heavenly father is vigorously stressed. The rabbis teach that God extends his fatherhood only to those who fulfil the Law (*Torah*). He is the father of those who do his will, of the just. Nevertheless, again and again the tremendous assurance of the prophets recurs that God's fatherly love is boundless and exceeds all human guilt. When Rabbi Jehuda (about AD 150) taught:

> *If you behave like children,*
> *you are called children;*
> *If you do not behave like children,*
> *you are not called children,*

his colleague and antagonist Rabbi Meir contradicted him with the bold, concise sentence:

> *Either way – you are called children.*[1]

God's fatherly love is his first and his last word, however great the children's guilt may be.

The second characteristic of Jewish statements of this period about God's fatherhood is that God is repeatedly spoken of as the father of the individual Israelite, and that he is addressed as father in liturgical prayers: *abhinu*,

[1] Babylonian Talmud, Tractate Qiddushim, 36a (Baraitha).

malkenu—'Our Father, our King'. Thus a prayer which could easily stem from the days of Jesus reads:

> *Our Father, our King,*
> *for the sake of our fathers*
> *who trusted upon thee*
> *and whom thou taughtest the statutes of life —*
> *have mercy upon us and teach us.*[1]

This is new as compared with the Old Testament. However, several things must not be overlooked here. First, Hebrew is used, the sacred language which was not employed in everyday speech. Second, the twin address, 'Our Father, our King', underscores God's majesty as a king as much as his fatherhood, or even more so. Third, it is the community as a whole which addresses God as 'our Father'.

To date nobody has produced one single instance in Palestinian Judaism where God is addressed as 'my Father' by an individual person.[2] There are a few examples in Hellenistic Judaism but these are due to Greek influence. From Palestinian writings, only one text may be quoted, namely two related verses from the twenty-third chapter of the Book of Sirach (beginning of the second century BC), which are, however, unfortunately only extant in Greek. Here we read, 'O Lord, Father and ruler of my life' (v. 1) and, 'O Lord, Father and God of my life'

---

[1] Prayer *Ahabha rabba*, the second of the benedictions which introduced the *Shema* as prayed every morning and evening. Presumably it was already part of the temple liturgy (Mishna, Tractate Tamid, 5.1). Text: W. B. Heidenheim, *Siddur Sephath Emeth*, Rödelheim, 1886, p. 17a. 13f.

[2] There are some isolated occurrences in *Sedher Eliyahu Rabba*, but this is a medieval composition (tenth century?) from South Italy.

(v. 4). These two verses would be the only exception to the rule, and we would praise them as a prelude to the Gospel, were it not that some thirty years ago a Hebrew paraphrase of this text was discovered. Here the address is not 'O Lord, Father' but 'O God of my father'.[1] It can hardly be doubted that this was the wording of the address in the original Hebrew text, for the designation of God as 'God of my father', stemming from Ex. 15.2, was widespread and occurs elsewhere in Sirach. This means that there is no evidence so far that in Palestinian Judaism of the first millennium anyone addressed God as 'my Father'.

3. 'Abba' in the Prayers of Jesus

But Jesus did just this. To his disciples it must have been something quite extraordinary that Jesus addressed God as 'my Father'. Moreover not only do the four Gospels attest that Jesus used this address, but they report unanimously that he did so in all his prayers.[2] There is only one prayer of Jesus in which 'my Father' is lacking. That is the cry from the cross: 'My God, my God, why hast thou forsaken me?' (Mark 15.34 par. Matt. 27.46), quoting Ps. 22.1.

Still, we have not yet said everything. The most remarkable thing is that when Jesus addressed God as his Father

[1] J. Marcus, 'A Fifth MS. of Ben Sira', *Jewish Quarterly Review* 21, 1930/31, 238.
[2] 21 times (16 times if parallels are counted only once).

in prayer he used the Aramaic word *abba*.[1] Mark states
this explicitly in his report on the prayer in Gethsemane:
'*Abba*, Father, all things are possible to thee; remove this
cup from me; yet not what I will, but what thou wilt'
(Mark 14.36). That Jesus used the same word *abba* in his
other prayers as well is proven by a comparison of the
different forms the address 'father' takes in Greek. Besides
the correct Greek vocative form '*pater*'[2] or '*pater mou*',[3] we
find the nominative '*ho patér*' used as a vocative which is
not correct Greek usage.[4] This oscillation between vocative and nominative which occurs even in one and the
same logion (Matt. 11.25, 26 par. Luke 10.21) cannot be
explained without taking into account that the word *abba*
—as we shall see presently—was current in first-century
Palestinian Aramaic not only as an address, but also for
'the father' (*status emphaticus*). Finally, besides Mark 14.36
and the variation of the address 'father' in Greek, we
have a third piece of evidence to prove that Jesus said
Abba when he prayed. It consists of two passages in Paul,
Rom. 8.15 and Gal. 4.6. They inform us that the Christian
communities used the cry '*Abba, ho patér*' ('Abba, Father')
and considered this an utterance brought forth by the
Holy Spirit. This applies to the Pauline (Galatians) as to
the non-Pauline (Romans) communities alike, and there
can be no doubt at all that this primitive Christian cry is
an echo of Jesus' own praying.

[1] The stress is on the final syllable.
[2] Matt. 11.25 par. Luke 10.21; Luke 11.2; 22.42; 23.34, 46;
John 11.41; 12.27f.; 17.1, 5, 11, 24, 25. [3] Matt. 26.39, 42.
[4] Mark 14.36; Matt. 11.26 par. Luke 10.21; Rom. 8.15; Gal. 4.6;
without the article only in variant readings: John 17.5, 11, 21, 24, 25.

This is without analogy in Jewish prayers of the first millennium AD. Nowhere in the literature of the prayers of ancient Judaism—an immense treasure all too little explored—is this invocation of God as *Abba* to be found, neither in the liturgical nor in the informal prayers.

There is only one passage in Late Jewish literature where the word *abba* is used in a certain connection with God. This is a story that relates an event which happened towards the end of the first century BC. It deals with Ḥanin ha-Neḥba, a man reputed for his successful prayers for rain, and reads:

> When the world was in need of rain, our teachers used to send the school children to him, who grasped the hem of his coat and implored him: '*Abba, abba, habh lan miṭra*, Daddy, Daddy, give us rain.' He said to Him (God): 'Master of the world, grant it (the rain) for the sake of these who are not yet able to distinguish between an *abba* who has the power to give rain, and an *abba* who has not.'[1]

At first sight it would seem as if here we have one instance in which God is called *Abba*. But two things must be observed. First, the word *abba* is applied to God in almost a joking manner. Ḥanin appeals to God's mercy by adopting the cry 'Daddy, Daddy, give us rain' which the children repeat after him in a chorus, calling God an '*Abba* who has the power to give rain', as children would in their own language. The second point is still more important. Ḥanin by no means addresses God as *Abba*. On the contrary, his address is 'Master of the world'. No doubt

[1] Babylonian Talmud, Tractate Ta'anith, 23b.

the story is something like a prelude to Jesus' assertion that the heavenly Father knows what his children need (Matt. 6.32 par.), that he sends rain on the just and the unjust (Matt. 5.45), and that he gives good things to his children who ask him (Matt. 7.11 par. Luke 11.13). But it does not give us the looked-for attestation of *abba* as an address to God. The fact remains unshaken that for this usage we have no evidence at all in Judaism.

This is a result of fundamental importance. Jewish prayers on the one hand do not contain a single example of *abba* as an address for God; Jesus on the other hand always used it when he prayed (with the exception of the cry from the cross, Mark 15.34). This means that we here have an unequivocal characteristic of the unique way in which Jesus expressed himself, of his *ipsissima vox*.

The reason why Jewish prayers do not address God as *Abba* is disclosed when one considers the linguistic background of the word. Originally, *abba* was a babbling sound. The Talmud says: 'When a child experiences the taste of wheat (that is, when it is weaned) it learns to say *abba* and *imma*' (that is, Dada and Mama are the first words which it utters);[1] and the church fathers Chrysostom, Theodore of Mopsuestia, and Theodoret of Cyrus, all three of them born in Antioch of well-to-do parents, but in all probability raised by Syrian nurses, tell us out of their own experience that little children used to call their fathers *abba*. When I started this study, which occupied me for quite a few years, I thought that it was just

[1] Babylonian Talmud, Tractate Berachoth, 40a (Bar.) par. Tractate Sanhedrin, 70b (Bar.).

this babbling sound which Jesus adopted. But very soon thereafter I noticed that this conclusion was too rash, for it overlooked the fact that already in pre-Christian times, this word, which surely originated from the idiom of the small child, had vastly extended its range of meaning in Palestinian Aramaic. *Abba* supplanted the older form *abhi* as an address to the father which was used in Palestinian Aramaic at least until the second century BC, as we have learned from the Scrolls. *Abba* furthermore took over the connotations of 'my father' and of 'the father'; it even occasionally replaced 'his father' and 'our father'. In this way, the word no longer remained restricted to the idiom of little children. Grown-up sons and daughters called their fathers *abba* as well (cp. Luke 15.21), and only on formal occasions resorted to 'Sir' (*Kyrie*) (cp. Matt. 21.29 [30]). But in spite of this development the origin of the word in the language of infants never falls into oblivion.

We are now in a position to say why *abba* is not used in Jewish prayers as an address to God: to a Jewish mind, it would have been irreverent and therefore unthinkable to call God by this familiar word.[1] It was something new, something unique and unheard of, that Jesus dared to take this step and to speak with God as a child speaks with his father, simply, intimately, securely. There is no doubt then that the *Abba* which Jesus uses to address God reveals the very basis of his communion with God.

[1] It is only in Hasidism (which originated in the eighteenth century) that we find God addressed in familiar ways (for instance, by diminutives), as was pointed out to the author by Dr Jacob Taubes of New York.

4. *The Fatherhood of God in the Gospels*

Is this childlike address to God to be regarded as a last stage in the general development of man's relation to God or is there more in it? We shall get an answer when we broaden our survey of the sources.

Until now, we have limited ourselves to the address of God as Father in the prayers of Jesus. We are led a step deeper when we turn to the sayings in which Jesus speaks of God as Father. That is to say, we turn our attention from the address 'my Father' to the designation of God as Father.

No less than one hundred and seventy times do we encounter in the Gospels the word Father for God in the mouth of Jesus. At first glance there does not appear to be the least doubt that for Jesus 'Father' was *the* designation for God. But is this really true? When we classify the texts according to the five strata of tradition represented in the gospels, the following pattern emerges (synoptic parallels are counted only once; the address 'Father' is excluded):

Mark	3 times
Sayings common to Matthew and Luke (so-called Logia-source)	4 ,,
Sayings special to Luke	4 ,,
Sayings special to Matthew	31 ,,
John	100 ,,

This survey shows that there existed an increasing tendency to introduce the designation of God as Father into the sayings of Jesus. Mark, the logia tradition, and the material peculiar to Luke all agree in reporting that Jesus used the word 'Father' for God only in a few instances. In Matthew there is a noticeable increase, and in John 'Father' has become almost a synonym for God. Apparently Jesus employed the name 'Father' only on special occasions. But why?

The few examples which the oldest strata of tradition record for the designation of God as Father fall into two classes: first a group in which Jesus speaks of God as 'your Father', and secondly a group in which Jesus calls him 'my Father'. The 'your Father' sayings picture God as the Father who knows what his children need (Matt. 6.32 par. Luke 12.30), who is merciful (Luke 6.36) and unlimited in goodness (Matt. 5.45), who can forgive (Mark 11.25), and whose good pleasure it is to grant the kingdom to the little flock (Luke 12.32). In the oldest strata of tradition these 'your Father' sayings seem to have been all addressed to the disciples. They are one characteristic of the *didache* (instruction) for the disciples, the esoteric teaching of Jesus. To those outside the circle Jesus seems to have spoken only in parables and similes about God as Father.

Of these esoteric sayings the most important is Matt. 11.27 par. Luke 10.22:

> *All things have been transmitted to me by my Father.*
> *And as only a father knows his son*
> *so also only a son knows his father*
> *and he to whom the son wants to reveal it.*

Karl von Hase, who a hundred years ago was professor of church history at Jena, in his book on the history of Jesus[1] coined the famous simile that this synoptic saying 'gives the impression of a thunderbolt fallen from the Johannine sky'. Two things above all in this text appeared Johannine: first, the phrase about mutual knowledge which was regarded as a technical term drawn from Hellenistic mysticism, and second, the designation of Jesus as 'the Son' which is characteristic of Johannine Christology. For a long time it was considered certain that Matt. 11.27 was a product of Hellenistic Christianity. However, not so long ago the tide began to turn. It was increasingly recognized that, as T. W. Manson put it, 'the passage is full of Semitic turns of phrase and certainly Palestinian in origin' or, as W. L. Knox said, it is 'purely Semitic'.[2] Indeed, language, style, and structure clearly assign the saying to a Semitic-speaking milieu.[3] The two objections just mentioned can be answered on simple linguistic grounds. Already in 1898 G. Dalman[4] drew attention to the fact that Hebrew and Aramaic lack the reciprocal

---

[1] *Die Geschichte Jesu*, second edition, Leipzig, 1876, 422.

[2] T. W. Manson, *The Sayings of Jesus*, London, 1937 = 1950, 79; W. L. Knox, *Some Hellenistic Elements in Primitive Christianity* (Schweich Lectures 1942), London, 1944, 7.

[3] W. D. Davies came to the same conclusion when he compared the role of 'knowledge' in Matt. 11.27 and in the Scrolls; he showed that in both cases we find the same combination of eschatological insight and knowledge of God (' "Knowledge" in the Dead Sea Scrolls and Matthew 11.25–30', *Harvard Theological Review*, 46, 1953, 113–139, reprinted in W. D. Davies, *Christian Origins and Judaism*, Philadelphia and London, 1962, 119–144).

[4] G. Dalman, *Die Worte Jesu* I, Leipzig, 1898 = ²1930, 231f. (Eng. trs., *The Words of Jesus* I, Edinburgh, 1902, 282f.).

pronoun ('one another', 'each other'). Instead they employ a roundabout way of expression when they want to describe reciprocal action. Further, we must remember that in Aramaic, especially in similes and comparisons, the definite article is quite often used in a generic sense. Taking these two facts into account, we must translate Matt. 11.27: 'As only a father knows his son, so only a son knows his father.' This means that the text neither speaks about a mystical union (*unio mystica*) brought about by mutual knowledge nor does it use the Christological title 'the Son'. Rather, Jesus' words simply express a plain, everyday experience: only father and son truly know each other. If this is true, then Matt. 11.27 is not a Johannine verse amidst the synoptic material, but rather one of those sayings from which Johannine theology developed. Without such points of departure within the synoptic tradition it would be an eternal puzzle how Johannine theology could have originated at all.

The saying Matt. 11.27 is a four-line couplet. The first line indicates the theme: 'All things have been transmitted to me by my Father.' My father has granted me full knowledge of him, says the first line. The three remaining lines elucidate this theme by means of the father-son comparison. Freely paraphrased, they say: 'And because only a father and a son truly know each other, therefore a son can reveal to others the innermost thoughts of his father.' Now one has to know that the father-son comparison is familiar to Palestinian apocalyptic as an illustration of how revelation is transmitted. 'Every secret did I reveal to him as a father,' God says in the Hebrew

(Third) Book of Enoch.[1] And in another passage a rabbi reports: The heavenly messenger showed me the things that were woven into the heavenly curtain'. . . by pointing with his finger as a father who teaches his son the letters of the Torah.'[2] So if Jesus interprets the theme 'all things have been transmitted to me by my Father' with the aid of this father-son comparison, what he wants to convey in the disguise of an everyday simile is this: As a father who personally devotes himself to explaining to his son the letters of the Torah, so God has transmitted to me the revelation of himself, and therefore I alone can pass on to others the real knowledge of God.

This saying in which Jesus bears witness to himself and his mission does not stand isolated in the Gospels.[3] Here we quote only a variant to Matt. 11.26 which was current in the second century among the Marcosians, a Gnostic sect, and which goes back to an old Aramaic tradition.[4] According to this reading Jesus cried out:

O my Father, that good pleasure was granted me before you!

This variant form of the exclamation in Matt. 11.26 may well be secondary. Nevertheless, it strikes the original note of Jesus' joy over the revelation granted to him, a joy which also permeates our text. 'O *Abba*, that good pleasure was granted me before you!'

Thus, when Jesus spoke of God as 'my Father' he was

[1] III Enoch 48(C).7.
[2] III Enoch 45.1f.
[3] Cp., for example, Mark 4.11; Matt. 11.25; Luke 10.23f.
[4] Irenaeus, *Adv. Haer.* I 13.2; W. Grundmann, *Die Geschichte Jesu Christi*, Berlin, 1956, 80.

referring not to a familiarity and intimacy with God available to anyone, but to a unique revelation which was bestowed upon him. He bases his authority on the fact that God has graciously endowed him with the full revelation, revealing himself to him as only a father can reveal himself to his son. *Abba*, then, is a word which conveys revelation. It represents the centre of Jesus' awareness of his mission (*Sendungsbewusstsein*).

If one looks for foreshadowings of this unique relation to God as Father one must go as far back as the prophecy given to Nathan concerning David: 'I will be his father, and he shall be my son' (II Sam. 7.14 par. I Chron. 17.13), and to words about the king in Ps. 2.7; 89.26f:

> *He shall cry to me, 'Thou art my Father,*
> *my God, and the Rock of my salvation.'*
> *And I will make him the first-born,*
> *the highest of the kings of the earth.*

From the Pseudepigrapha we may quote the promise given to the priestly Messiah, that God would speak to him 'with a fatherly voice' (Testament of Levi 18.6) and the affirmation extending to the Messiah from Judah that 'the blessings of the holy father' shall be poured out over him (Testament of Judah 24.2). This means that this 'my Father' of Jesus is foreshadowed only within the context of the messianic expectation. Matt. 11.27 then implies that these promises were fulfilled in Jesus.

5. *The Lord's Prayer*

It is only against this background that we can understand the deepest meaning of the Lord's Prayer.[1]

It is handed down to us in two forms (*a*) the shorter one in Luke 11.2–4, and (*b*) the longer one in Matt. 6.9–13. Whereas nobody would have dared to shorten this central text, it is easy to conceive of an expansion of the text in conjunction with its liturgical usage. The shorter Lucan version must then be the older one. Here the address is simply *pater*, the equivalent of *Abba*.

In order to understand what this address meant for the disciples, we have to refer to the situation in which Jesus gave his disciples the Our Father. According to Luke 11.1 they had asked: 'Lord, teach us to pray.' One is to recognize that this request implied the desire of the disciples to have a prayer of their own, just as the followers of the Baptist, the Pharisees and the Essenes had their own prayers, tokens of their communion. 'Lord, teach us to pray' means then: 'Lord, give us a prayer which will be the sign and token of your followers.'

Jesus fulfils this request, and in so doing he first and foremost authorizes his disciples to follow him in saying *Abba*. He gives them this address as the token of their discipleship. By the authorization that they, too, may invoke God as *Abba*, he lets them participate in his own

[1] Cp. for fuller treatment my study, 'The Lord's Prayer in Modern Research', *Expository Times* 71, 1959/1960, 141–146; revised form, *The Lord's Prayer* (Facet Books, Biblical Series 8), Philadelphia, 1964.

communion with God. He even goes as far as to say that only he who can repeat this childlike *Abba* shall enter into the kingdom of God.[1] This address, *Abba*, when spoken by the disciples, is a sharing in the revelation, it is actualized eschatology. It is the presence of the kingdom even here, even now. It is a fulfilment, granted in advance, of the promise:

> *I shall be their father*
> *and they my children.*
> *They all shall be called children of the living God.*
>
> (Jubilees 1.24f.)

This is the way Paul understood the address when he says twice that it is proof of the possession of sonship and of the Spirit, when a Christian repeats this one word *Abba* (Rom. 8.15; Gal. 4.6). The ancient Christian liturgies show their awareness of the greatness of this gift in that they preface the Lord's Prayer with the words: 'We *make bold* to say: "Our Father".'

6. Conclusion

With all this we are facing a conclusion of fundamental importance.

It has been widely maintained that we know scarcely anything about the historical Jesus. We know him only from the Gospels, which are not historical accounts but

[1] J. Jeremias, *The Parables of Jesus*, revised edition, London and New York, 1963, 190f.

rather confessions of faith. We know only the Christ of the Kerygma, where Jesus is clad in the garb of myth; one need only think of the many miracles attributed to him. What we discover, when we apply historical criticism in analysing the sources, is a powerful prophet, but a prophet who completely remained within the limits of Judaism. This prophet may have historical interest, but he has not and cannot have any significance for the Christian faith. What matters is the Christ of the Kerygma. Christianity began at Easter.

But if it is true—and the testimony of the sources is quite unequivocal—that *Abba* as an address to God is *ipsissima vox*, an authentic and original utterance of Jesus, and that this *Abba* implies the claim of a unique revelation and a unique authority—if all this is true, then the position regarding the historical Jesus just described is untenable. For with *Abba* we are behind the Kerygma. We are confronted with something new and unheard of which breaks through the limits of Judaism. Here we see who the historical Jesus was: the man who had the power to address God as *Abba* and who included the sinners and the publicans in the kingdom by authorizing them to repeat this one word, '*Abba*, dear Father'.

TWO

The Sacrificial Death

1. The Atonement in Hebrews and I Peter

OF ALL New Testament writings, the Letter to the Hebrews provides us with the most extensive interpretation of the cross. This letter, actually the oldest Gentile Christian sermon preserved (13.22), distinguishes between elementary instruction (the 'first principles' 5.12) and deeper knowledge (called 'maturity' in 6.1), in other words, between exoteric and esoteric teaching. The former contained instruction about baptism and the end of the times; it was, in short, the substance of what catechumens had to learn (cp. Heb. 6.1f.). Esoteric teaching, on the other hand, concerns itself with the Eucharist[1] and, above all, with the doctrine of the self-sacrifice of Christ, the heavenly high priest. The explanation of this doctrine forms the central part of the letter (7.1–10.18).

[1] This may be inferred from the fact that the Eucharist is lacking in 6.2 where the subjects of pre-baptismal teaching are enumerated.

In order to illustrate the saving power of Christ's death, Hebrews draws upon the ritual for the Day of Atonement, celebrated on 10 Tishri every autumn, as laid down in Lev. 16. The Day of Atonement, Israel's great day of repentance and reconciliation, was the only day during the entire year on which a human being was allowed to enter the Holy of Holies. Trembling, because even a minor deviation from the prescribed ritual would entail a terrible death, the high priest penetrated into the darkness behind the curtain to offer that precious blood which was to remove all sins. The Letter to the Hebrews makes this ritual a type of the atoning work of Christ in two ways. First (here Hebrews is dependent upon traditional ideas), Christ is compared to the faultless victim, who through his vicarious death assures forgiveness and full communion with God. Secondly, elaborating an expression from Ps. 110.4, Hebrews also depicts Christ as the eternal, sinless high priest who, having atoned for sin once and for all, remains perpetually in the presence of God and intercedes with sympathy for his people (7.25; 9.24, cp. 2.18; 4.14–16).

This Christology of Hebrews is a very impressive attempt to lead the Church to an understanding of the mystery of the cross by means of a typological interpretation of Lev. 16. Stripped of its imagery, this interpretation means: Good Friday is *the* Day of Atonement of the New Covenant, of which all the Days of Atonement, repeated year after year, were but types and patterns. The benefits of this new, and final, Day of Atonement are twofold. First, Christ's vicarious sinless death answers man's cry for forgiveness— once and for all (7.27; 9.12; 10.10). Secondly, actualizing this reconciliation, Christ, himself tempted and afflicted while on earth, intercedes in heaven for his tempted and afflicted Church.

When we turn to I Peter we find that quite different imagery is used to interpret Jesus' death, namely the doctrine of Christ's descent into and preaching in Hades (3.19f.; 4.6). In order to understand this doctrine, it must be observed that it has an antitype in the Ethiopic Book of Enoch, which received its present shape after the invasion of Palestine by the Parthians in 37 BC. Chapters 12–16 of this book describe how Enoch is sent to the fallen angels of Gen. 6 to convey to them the message that they will 'find no peace and no forgiveness'. Stricken with terror, they ask Enoch to draw up a petition in which they implore God's indulgence and forgiveness. Enoch is then lifted up to God's fiery throne and receives God's answer which he must dispatch to the fallen sons of God. It consists of one short clause of five words only, the terrible sentence: 'You will have no peace.'

It can hardly be doubted that the doctrine of Christ's descent into Hades is modelled upon this myth from the book of Enoch. But whereas Enoch's message spells out the impossibility of forgiveness, Christ announces something different: the good news (I Peter 4.6). 'The righteous one died for the unrighteous' (3.18). His atoning death means salvation even for those who were hopelessly lost.

Both the Letter to the Hebrews and the First Epistle of Peter intend to elucidate what happened on Good Friday, but in doing so they resort to utterly different illustrations. Hebrews speaks of Jesus *ascending* into Heaven in order to

33

offer his blood in the heavenly Holy of Holies, whereas I
Peter speaks of Jesus *descending* into the blackest depths of
Hades in order to preach to the 'spirits in prison'. Ascent
and descent are two parallel attempts to bring out the
meaning of Good Friday. The two representations are
different from each other (Hebrews using cultic, I Peter
mythological imagery); as far as the local aspect is concerned, they even stand opposed to each other. This is a
wholesome warning against overestimating the importance
of the imagery involved. What matters is the point at which
they agree. Both wish to express one and the same message:
the atoning power of Jesus' death is inexhaustible and
boundless.

2. *Paul*

Both Hebrews and I Peter reveal themselves as in many
ways dependent upon the theology of Paul. It is to his
letters, then, that we now have to turn our attention as we
trace our way back through the New Testament. Here we
meet with a new situation. It is not as though Paul had
something to say about Christ's death which differs in
content from the post-Pauline writings. On the contrary,
the stability of content in spite of varying forms is one of
the most prominent characteristics of our subject throughout the New Testament. The difference between Paul and,
let us say, the Letter to the Hebrews is not one of opinion,
but of atmosphere. Hebrews endeavours to explain and

amplify the mystery of the cross by a profound and well-balanced array of typological arguments, the fruit of an intensive theological reflection. On the other hand, when we read what Paul writes about the same subject, we still get a feeling of how he had to wrestle with the problem of getting this much debated core of his message across to his hearers. Let me illustrate this by an example which gives us a glimpse of how the interpretation of the cross, later a firmly established part of the Church's tradition, had to be intensely fought for in the beginning. I mean Gal. 3.13: 'Christ became a curse for us,' or rather (if we observe that 'became' is a circumlocution for the action of God, and that 'curse' is a metonym for 'the cursed one') 'God made Christ a cursed one for our sake.' This sentence from Galations—in which Paul applies Deut. 21.23 ('A hanged man is accursed by God') to Christ—is so familiar to us that we no longer sense its original offensiveness. We should, perhaps, if we noted that not one other New Testament writer ever dared utter anything which even remotely resembles this statement of Paul's. The only explanation of this shocking phrase 'God made Christ a cursed one' is that it originated in the time before the episode on the Damascus road.[1] Jesus of Nazareth, a man ostensibly accursed by God—that was why Saul persecuted him in the guise of his followers, why he blasphemed him (I Tim. 1.13) and tried to compel blasphemy from his disciples (Acts 26.11), namely the cry: *Anathema Jesus*—'Jesus be

[1] First seen by P. Feine, *Das gesetzesfreie Evangelium des Paulus*, Leipzig, 1899, 18. The point has been taken up again recently and enforced by Gert Jeremias, *Der Lehrer der Gerechtigkeit*, Göttingen, 1963, 134f.

cursed' (I Cor. 12.3). But then, on the Damascus road, the accursed one appeared before Paul in divine glory. After this experience, Paul still went on saying 'God made Christ a cursed one', but now he added two words: 'for us' or 'for me' (Gal. 2.20). From now on 'for us' was to be the heart of his existence. By an increasing number of comparisons and images, he tries to make his hearers and readers understand the meaning of this 'for us', i.e. the idea of Christ's vicarious death. Among them, four themes may easily be identified.

First, there is the cultic theme which was suggested to Paul by Christian tradition. In I Cor. 5.7 he says: 'You are free from leaven. For Christ has been sacrificed as our Passover lamb.' To be a Christian, Paul says, is to live at Passover time, to stand in the light of Easter morning, in a new life—this Passover began when our Passover lamb was sacrificed on Calvary. Along with this comparison of Christ to the Passover lamb—also found in I Peter and the Gospel of John—Paul uses other comparisons drawn from cultic language. Thus, in Rom. 3.25, he compares Christ with the sacrifice offered on the Day of Atonement; in Rom. 8.3 with the sin-offering; in Eph. 5.2 with the burnt offering. In each case the treatment of Jesus' death in terms of sacrifice has the intention of expressing the fact that Jesus died without sin in substitution for our sins. His death is the sum and the end of all sacrifices prescribed by the Old Testament ritual. It is the one sacrifice for the sins of all mankind.

A second theme used by Paul to illustrate how Christ took our place is borrowed from criminal law. All those passages referring to Isa. 53, the chapter about the Suffering Servant who carried the punishment inflicted because of our transgressions, belong here, as for instance Rom. 4.25 ('He was delivered for our offences'). A particularly impressive image illustrating how Christ suffered the death penalty which we deserved is used in Col. 2.14: 'God has cancelled the writ issued against us which enumerated the statutes we had violated, and destroyed it by nailing it to the cross.' When a man was crucified there was affixed over his head a tablet—the so-called *titulus*—which he had carried around his neck on his way to the place of execution. The crimes for which he had been sentenced were inscribed on this *titulus*. Above Jesus' head also hangs a *titulus*. 'But don't you see', says Paul, 'that there is a hand which removes this *titulus* and replaces it with another one, with lines of writing crowded upon it? You will have to draw near if you want to decipher this new *titulus*—it is your sins and mine that are inscribed upon it.'

Besides the cultic and the legal themes there is a third one which Paul has taken from the institution of slavery. The key words are 'to buy' (I Cor. 6.20; 7.23), 'to redeem' (Gal. 3.13; 4.5), 'with a price' (I Cor. 6.20; 7.23). Christ redeemed us from slavery through his death. What Paul means is the dramatic act of entering into slavery in order to redeem a slave. It is this self-sacrifice out of love to which Paul alludes when he says in I Cor. 13.3: 'If I give away all I have, and if I deliver my body to be burned (that is, branded with the slave-mark), but have not love, I gain nothing.' We know from the *First Letter of Clement* (AD 96) that such extreme expressions of brotherly love did in fact occur in the primitive Church (55.2). That, says Paul, is what Christ did for us. We were slaves of sin (Rom. 3.9 *et al.*), of the law (Gal. 4.5), of God's curse (Gal. 3.13). The crucified Lord took our place as a slave of these powers in order to redeem us legitimately (I Cor. 6.20; 7.23). To grasp the wonderful ring which the word 'redemption' had in the ears of the slaves who belonged to the earliest Christian communities, we must be mindful of the terrible condition of slaves in antiquity who were helplessly exposed to the whims and caprices of their masters and were forced to work themselves to death in mines or on the galleys.

The last of our four themes is the ethical substitution consisting in Christ's vicarious obedience, of which—if I am not mistaken—there are only two occurrences. The first is Rom. 5.18f. Here, in two antithetic phrases of similar structure, Paul contrasts the universal effects of Adam's transgression with Christ's act of obedience: 'Through the obedience of this one man (i.e. because he kept in our place the commandments which we should have kept) the many will become righteous.' The second instance is Gal. 4.4f.: 'Christ became a slave of the law in order to redeem those who were slaves of the law (that is, by fulfilling the law where they should have done it) so that we might receive the sonship.'

The images may be different, but one and the same intention underlies these four themes: Paul wants to illustrate the 'for us', the sinless one taking the place of the sinners. He takes the very place of the ungodly (Rom. 5.6), of the enemies of God (5.10), of the world opposed to God (II Cor. 5.19). In this way the boundless omni-potence of God's all-inclusive love reveals itself (Rom. 5.8). Christ's vicarious death on the cross is the actualization of God's love.

3. *The Primitive Church*

Going back one step further, we now direct our attention to the primitive Church before Paul. Here the difficulty arises that the primitive Church has left us no written statements. And yet we may say with certainty that the interpretation of the meaning of the cross was a point of major concern even for the first Christian community. From the very day of Easter the historical situation forced them to give an answer to the mystery of the cross.

To the ancients the cross was the symbol not only of the most horrible sufferings, but also of utmost infamy (Heb. 12.2). In addition, as we have seen, Jewish sentiment concluded from Deut. 21.23 that this form of capital punishment, unknown to Israel, was a token of God's curse. How then could it happen that he whom God had acknowledged through the resurrection should have died under God's curse? The archaic confession, I Cor. 15.3, shows where the answer was found: 'Christ died for our sins according to the scriptures.' The phrase 'for our sins' implies that his death was a vicarious one, while 'according to the scriptures' backs this interpretation of Jesus' death with Isa. 53—it is the only chapter in the Old Testament that contains a statement corresponding to 'he died for our sins'

It will always remain difficult for me to understand how it could have been doubted that I Cor. 15.3 alludes to Isa. 53. At least no appeal should have been made to the plural 'the scriptures'. It has been argued that this plural cannot mean Isa. 53 because it refers to a multitude of scriptural passages, not just one. This, however, is a philological error. The Greek plural 'the scriptures' goes back to a similar Aramaic term which is just another expression for 'the Bible', as 'the Scriptures' is in English today. Besides, there are other proofs that the early Church has applied Isa. 53 to Jesus. Such references abound in Paul's writings. Now it is an impressive fact that not one of these has been coined by Paul himself; all without exception are drawn from pre-Pauline tradition. This can be shown in some cases by style, in other cases by vocabulary, in most cases by both.[1] Thus, it cannot reasonably be doubted that even in its earliest days the Church found in the chapter about the Suffering Servant the key to the dark riddle why the Son of God had to die under God's curse.

4. *Jesus' Interpretation of His Death*

The Gospels report that this interpretation of Jesus' death goes back to Jesus himself. But can they be trusted?

One thing seems certain to me: the events during Jesus'

[1] Detailed evidence (which could be amplified) in: W. Zimmerli and J. Jeremias, *The Servant of God* (Studies in Biblical Theology 20), London, 1957, 88f., 95f. (revised edition, London, 1965, *ibid.*)

ministry must have forced him to reckon more and more with the inevitability of his own persecution, and even a violent death. He had been reproached with transgression of the Sabbath, with blasphemy and with magic (Mark 3.22b). In each case the crime entailed the punishment of death by stoning[1] with subsequent hanging of the dead body.[2] Furthermore, Jesus repeatedly reckoned himself among the prophets (such sayings stand a good chance of being authentic because of the seemingly modest Christology they imply). Now in his days martyrdom was considered an integral part of the prophetic ministry; this fact is confirmed by the New Testament, the contemporary legends about the prophets, and the custom of honouring the prophets' tombs with monuments in expiation of their murder, a custom which came into vogue during Jesus' lifetime (Matt. 23.29; Luke 11.47) and to which the great monuments in the Kidron Valley still bear witness today.[3] Jesus himself shared this view of the prophetic ministry and was convinced that the prophetic destiny awaited him also (Luke 13.33). He considered the history of salvation as an uninterrupted sequence of martyred saints from Abel to Zechariah, the son of Jehoiada (Matt. 23.35), and he particularly took the fate of the last in the line, John the Baptist, as a hint of what awaited him (Mark 9.11–13).

Under these circumstances, we can only expect that Jesus spoke to his disciples about the fate which he foresaw as the Gospels tell us. But here we must not overlook an

[1] Mishna, Tractate Sanhedrin, 7.4.
[2] *Ibid.*, 6.4 (R. Eliezer).
[3] J. Jeremias, *Heiligengräber in Jesu Umwelt*, Göttingen, 1958.

41

important fact. For in speaking of Jesus' predictions of his passion, we usually think only of the direct announcements (Mark 8.31; 9.31; 10.33f. and parallels), which, by the way, are really three variants of one and the same announcement. But besides these plain and direct announcements, we have a great number of indirect announcements, which form the older and more important layer of tradition. I think that it has been a source of error that critical investigation has focused almost exclusively on the direct announcements. It is true that when we analyse these direct announcements of Jesus' passion along the lines of literary criticism we do observe a marked tendency of the Gospel tradition to put such statements into Jesus' mouth (thus Matt. 26.2, cp. Mark 14.1), and in addition a tendency to assimilate such statements step by step to the historic course of events. These tendencies cannot be doubted, and it is easy to understand why many scholars have concluded from these that all of Jesus' announcements of his passion and resurrection which have come down to us are *vaticinia ex eventu*—that they have all been created after the events they purport to predict. Actually, this conclusion is untenable. Even the most critical analysis of the direct announcements—leaving aside for the moment the indirect predictions—cannot but reveal a core in Jesus' sayings about his passion which must antedate the crucifixion.

Undoubtedly, the kernel of the direct announcements belongs to the pre-Hellenistic stratum of tradition. That is shown for instance by the play on words which appears when Mark 9.31 is retranslated into Aramaic: God will surrender the man (*bar naša*) in the hands of men (*bᵉne naša*). It is also shown by the fact that these announcements almost never refer to the Greek text of the Old Testament but rather to the Hebrew text. Still weightier is the observation that the first of them (Mark 8.31) is so closely connected with its context, the rebuke of Peter, that it cannot be separated from it; this means that this announcement shares the claim to authenticity which must be attributed to Peter's designation as Satan in Mark 8.33.[1] Finally, this pre-Easter nucleus of the plain announcements becomes evident when we examine the phrase 'after three days'. At first glance, it seems probable that the sentence in Mark 8.31 par. 'and after three days he will rise again' is entirely formulated *ex eventu*—after the events. But there are additional sayings referring to three days. After three days, Jesus affirms, he will build the New Temple (Mark 14.58 and par.). He casts out demons and performs cures today and tomorrow, and the third day he will be perfected (Luke 13.32). A little while, and they will see him no more; again a little while, and they will see him again: today they have fellowship with him, tomorrow they will be separated, the third day the parousia will take place (John 16.16). It is quite clear that Jesus announced in various ways God's great triumph which was to change the world in three days—i.e. after a short while. In all these 'three days' sayings there is nowhere a distinction between the resurrection and the parousia. That, if nothing else, shows already that the substance of such announcements antedates Easter.

[1] Cp. Zimmerli and Jeremias, *op. cit.*, 103 (rev. ed., 104).

With these last remarks, we have already touched upon the indirect predictions of the passion, which are the more important ones because they have not been submitted to a reshaping equal to that of the direct announcements. These indirect announcements are very numerous and represent a broad variety of literary forms. There are similes (like chalice, baptism, ransom, the slain shepherd) and parables (like the wicked husbandmen), there are riddle-sayings (so-called *mešalim*, like the one about Jonah or about the need of swords, as well as others), there are menacing sayings (like Luke 13.32), there are the many announcements of the passion of the disciples, there are the words of interpretation spoken at the last Supper. This great variety shows that these indirect announcements are deeply rooted in the tradition. Even more significant is the fact that they contain a number of features which were not borne out literally by the subsequent events. For instance, Jesus seems to have thought it possible that he would be buried as a criminal (Mark 14.8), an indignity which was spared him, and that some of his disciples would have to share his fate (Mark 10.32–40; Luke 14.25–33; 22.36f.), which did not happen immediately; strangely enough, the authorities were content with executing Jesus and left his disciples alone.

Accumulated evidence of this kind forbids us to declare Jesus' announcements unauthentic *in toto*. Scepticism involuntarily turns into falsification of history if it allows itself to be carried away by individual critical observations, right as they may be, into attributing the whole of the material uncritically to the faith of the early Church.

Now if it be admitted that the substance of Jesus' announcements of his passion and of his glorification goes back to the Lord himself, then one has no right lightly to discard those texts which assert that Jesus not only announced but also interpreted his passion and to regard them as dogmas of the early Church. Quite the opposite! Whoever is even faintly familiar with the extraordinary importance which the idea of the atoning power of suffering and death had attained in Late Judaism will have to admit that it is completely inconceivable that Jesus would have expected to suffer and die without having reflected on the meaning of these events.

Among the texts in question, first of all attention must be drawn to the Eucharistic Words. What matters here are the words 'for many'. I will restrict myself to two remarks. In the first place, these words are preserved in all versions of the Words of Institution which the New Testament hands down to us, although with some variations as to position and phrasing. Mark 14.24 says 'for many', Matt. 26.28 'on behalf of many', I Cor. 11.24 and Luke 22.19, 20 have 'for you', and finally John 6.51 writes 'for the life of the world'. Of the different versions of this expression, Mark's 'for many', being a Semitism, is older than Paul's and Luke's 'for you'. Since Paul is likely to have received his formulation of the Eucharistic Words in the beginning of the forties in Antioch,[1] Mark's 'for many' leads us back into the first decade after Jesus' death. Whoever wishes to drop those two words as a secondary comment ought to realize that he is abandoning a very

[1] Cp. my book, *The Eucharistic Words of Jesus*, Oxford, 1955, 131.

45

ancient piece of tradition and that there are no linguistic grounds on which he can stand. In the second place, the words 'for many' are a reference to Isa. 53, as Mark 10.45 confirms. The idea of substitution as well as the word 'many' alludes to just this passage, for 'many' without the article, in the inclusive sense of 'the many', 'the great number', 'all', abounds in Isa. 53[1] and constitutes something like the keyword of this chapter. Thus, the phrase 'for many' in the Eucharistic Words shows that Jesus found the key to the meaning of his passion and death in Isa. 53.

A saying closely related to the Eucharistic Words is the logion about ransom, Mark 10.45 (par. Matt. 20.28). The history of its tradition is more complicated than that of the Eucharistic Words, because Mark and Matthew differ from Luke 22.27. Whereas Mark and Matthew read: 'The Son of Man came not to be served, but to serve, and to give his life as a ransom for many,' Luke has: 'Which is the greater, one who sits at table, or one who serves? Is it not the one who sits at table? But I am among you as one who serves.' What can be made of this seems to be that behind both versions there lies a saying in which Jesus spoke of himself as a servant. In the source peculiar to Luke this service is illustrated by Jesus' waiting at table, in Mark by means of Isa. 53. In Luke the context is strongly Hellenized as far as the language is concerned, whereas in Mark not only the language but also the imagery is Semitic, for the religious application of the

[1] 'Many' as a substantive without article: Isa. 52.14; 53.12e. LXX presupposes the word without article also in 53.11c, 12a.

simile of ransom is typically Palestinian. The least that must be said with regard to this saying is this: besides the Eucharistic Words, Mark had one more piece of ancient tradition which presents Jesus as interpreting his passion with the aid of Isa. 53.

We meet another very old tradition in the saying about the swords, Luke 22.35–38, which comes from Luke's special source. I would venture to say that here we once more strike the bed-rock of tradition. Jesus warns his disciples that the attitude of their compatriots towards them is going to shift abruptly from friendship and hospitality to fierce hatred. The peaceful times are past and gone. By all means, buy swords. The reason for this radical change is given by a quotation from Isa. 53.12: 'He was reckoned with transgressors.' Jesus' passion will also mark the turning point of the fate of his followers. As soon as we realize that what Jesus announces is not just hatred and persecution but the immediately imminent beginning of the apocalyptic tribulation, it is evident that we are dealing with a saying which cannot have been coined *ex eventu* but must be pre-Easter. In v. 38 there follows another very ancient saying, that of the disciples: 'Here there are two swords.' It must be ancient because it admits without concealing or glossing over the disciples' utter lack of understanding. Again it is Isa. 53 which furnishes in Luke 22.35–38 the interpretation of the passion lying before Jesus.

No doubt we must also regard Mark 14.27f., the saying about the shepherd who is slain and whose sheep are scattered, as belonging to pre-Easter tradition. The reason why it must be so old lies in v. 28 where Jesus says: 'But after I am raised up, I will go before you to Galilee.' The decisive point is that 'to go before' is shepherd-language. That means that the promise that Jesus will go before his disciples to Galilee is still part of the simile of the shepherd. Now, the image of the shepherd preceding his flock and guiding them to Galilee can by no means have been worded *ex eventu* after the resurrection. Rather this image condenses Zech. 13.7–9 where it says that the death of the shepherd ushers in not only the eschatological tribulation of the flock but also the gathering of the tried and purified remnant within the kingdom of God (cp. Zech. 14.9). Again, as in Luke 22.35–38, it is Jesus' death which marks the turning-point inaugurating the final tribulation and salvation. John 10, where the simile of the slain shepherd is taken up, stresses the vicarious significance of his death (v. 11, 15) in terms reminiscent of Isa. 53.

Finally, mention must be made of Luke 23.34, Jesus' intercession on the cross: 'Father, forgive them; for they know not what they do.' This prayer is an addition to the oldest text but one that is based on ancient tradition, as both the form (God being addressed as 'Father', *Abba*) and the context (the intercession for the enemies) show. Again we have in this prayer an implicit interpretation of Jesus' death. For Jesus offers it in place of the expiatory vow: 'May my death expiate all my sins,' which a condemned man had to say before his execution. Jesus applies the atoning virtue of his death not to himself, as was the custom, but to his executioners. Here again Isa. 53 is in the

background, closing with the words: 'and he made intercession for the transgressors' (v. 12).

All five texts were of great importance for the Church
and were connected with her life: the Words of Institution
with her Eucharist; the ransom-saying Mark 10.45 with
her ethical instruction; Luke 23.34 with her life of prayer
(cp. Acts 7.60); Luke 22.35–38 and Mark 14.27f. with both
her handing down of the tradition about Jesus' passion and
her own tribulations.

The number of instances where Jesus applies Isa. 53 to
himself is limited. The reason is that Jesus unveiled the
deepest mysteries of his mission only to his disciples and
not in his public teaching. Judaism in Jesus' time confirms
this fact, showing us that the deepest meaning of the gathering of an inner circle of disciples was that they alone could
share in the last insights of the master.[1] Thus, Jesus let only
his disciples share the secret that he considered the fulfilment of Isa. 53 the task put before him by God; only to
them did he interpret his death as a vicarious action in substitution for the 'many', the countless number of those who
were bound to be condemned by God. According to Isa. 53
there are four reasons why the death of the Servant of God
has such unlimited atoning power: his passion is voluntary
(v. 10), patiently undergone (v. 7), in accordance with
God's will (vv. 6, 10) and innocent (v. 9). It is life from
God and with God that is here put to death.

If we have succeeded in tracing the primitive Christian

---

[1] It is one of the merits of the late T. W. Manson to have stressed
the importance of the esoteric teaching of Jesus in his book, *The
Teaching of Jesus*, second edition, Cambridge, 1935.

interpretation of Jesus' death as a fulfilment of Isa. 53 back to Jesus himself with great probability—certainty is not to be expected at this point—we are still faced with the existential question whether all this is true, whether his death on Calvary was just one of the many martyrs' deaths which history records or whether it was the one vicarious death which atones for the sins of the world. This question remains. However, the answer to this decisive question is now entrusted not to the Church, but to Jesus himself.

THREE

Justification by Faith

1. The Meaning of the Formula

IN AN introductory paragraph, I should like to lay the foundation for what follows by making some linguistic observations. We ask: what is meant by (*a*) to be justified, (*b*) by faith, (*c*) of grace?

Like the Hebrew verb *ṣadhaq*, *dikaioun* in the Septuagint belongs to legal terminology. In the active, it means 'to do a man justice', 'to declare a man innocent', 'to acquit a defendant'. Accordingly, the passive meaning is 'to win in court', 'to be declared innocent', 'to be acquitted'. In this sense, *dikaioun* is also used in the New Testament, cp. Matt. 12.37, a reference to the Last Judgment: 'By your words you will be acquitted (*dikaiôthêsê*), and by your words you will be condemned.' The same contrast 'to acquit' 'to condemn' also occurs in Rom. 8.33f., a quotation from Isa. 50.8: 'It is God who acquits (*theos ho dikaiôn*); who is to condemn?' All this can be read in any lexicon.

However, it must be noted that the verb *dikaioun/*

dikaiousthai had undergone an extension of its range of meaning, specifically when it was used of God's action. The new shade of meaning is first found in Deutero-Isaiah. Isa. 45.25 reads in the Septuagint:

> *From the Lord shall be justified* (dikaiôthêsetai)
> *and by God shall be glorified*
> *all the offspring of Israel.*

In this saying Deutero-Isaiah clearly breaks through the bounds of the forensic usage. The parallelism between 'to be justified' and 'to be glorified' demonstrates that *dikaiousthai* here assumes the meaning 'to find salvation'.

As far as I know, it has not yet been noted that this usage lived on in post-biblical Judaism. At least two instances can be adduced. In Pseudo-Philo's *Biblical Antiquities* (written after AD 70) 'to be justified' appears as a parallel to God's election (49.4), and similarly in Fourth Ezra (written AD 94), 'to find grace', 'to be justified' and 'to be heard in prayer' are used as synonyms (12.7).

The last-mentioned passage is the beginning of a prayer. It reads:

> *O most high Lord,*
> *If I have found grace in your eyes*
> *and if I have been justified in your presence before many*
> *and if my prayer assuredly rises to your countenance . . .*

The last three lines are in parallelism. In the first and second of these 'to find grace' alternates with 'to be justified' without any apparent change of meaning. Therefore the literal translation, 'to be justified', is too

52

narrow and does not get at the heart of the expression. Rather, what the text intends is:

If I have found grace in your eyes
and if I have found good pleasure in your presence before
  many . . .

What is important here is that the idea of a trial in court has been abandoned. 'To be justified', as applied to an act of God and parallel to 'to find grace', does not have the narrow meaning 'to be acquitted', but rather the more extensive one 'to find good pleasure'. This is confirmed by the third parallel line, which indicates how God's grace, his good pleasure, is expressed: it consists in his hearing the prayer.

All this brings us within close reach of a saying from the Gospels, namely Luke 18.14, where Jesus says about the publican: 'I tell you, this man went down to his house justified, and not the other.' Here, too, the forensic comparison is abandoned. Here, too, 'to be justified' rather has the meaning 'to find God's good pleasure'. Here, too, this good pleasure of God manifests itself in that he hears prayer. Luke 18.14, then, has to be rendered accordingly: 'I tell you, this man went down to his house as one who had found God's good pleasure, and not the other.' We may even go so far as to translate this: 'I tell you, this man went down to his house as one whose prayer God had heard, and not the other.'

We have thus encountered a use of *dikaiousthai* in which the forensic comparison seems to have been watered down or even completely abandoned. I should like to call this usage 'soteriological' to distinguish it from the forensic usage.

It is obvious that in Paul, too, the use of 'to justify' (or 'to be justified') reaches far beyond the legal sphere. Even though the forensic aspect is by no means lacking—we have already mentioned the hymn-like ending of Rom. 8 where Paul (in vv. 33f.) uses the figure of the court trial in quoting Isa. 50.8: 'It is God who acquits (*dikaiôn*); who is to condemn?'—the soteriological connotation governs his speech. For Paul, the active *dikaioun* means 'to grant grace or good pleasure', the passive *dikaiousthai*, 'to find grace or good pleasure'. That the figure of court proceedings is absent becomes especially apparent where Paul talks about a justification that lies in the past, as, for instance, in Rom. 4.2: 'If Abraham found grace (*edikaiôthê*) by works . . .' Here in the story of Abraham's faith we are not dealing with a forensic scene but rather with a bestowing of God's grace. The same is true of 5.1: 'Therefore, since we have found grace (*dikaiôthentes*) by faith, we have peace with God'; and of 5.9: 'Since we have found grace (*dikaiôthentes*) by his blood'. God's justification is an outpouring of grace which far exceeds the legal sphere.

With regard to the substantive *dikaiosynê* (*tou*) *theou* the soteriological connotation has been noted long ago, first, to my knowledge, by James Hardy Ropes at the beginning of this century.[1] In the Psalms and in Deutero-Isaiah *ṣidhqath Jahwe*, 'God's righteousness', is used alternately with God's salvation, God's mercy. This is precisely Paul's

[1] 'Righteousness in the Old Testament and in St Paul', *Journal of Biblical Literature* 22, 1903, 211–227.

usage (with the exception of Rom. 3.5 where, however, he is not speaking himself, but quoting an objection). Thus, for example, Rom. 1.17 must not be rendered: 'In the gospel the righteousness of God is revealed,' but 'In the gospel God's salvation is revealed.'

In summary: as in the Pauline letters *dikaiosynê (tou) theou* must be translated, 'God's salvation', so *dikaiousthai* must be rendered, 'to find God's grace'.

Now we may turn to the words *pistei, ek pisteôs, dia pisteôs*, 'by faith'. Whenever Paul speaks of God's *dikaiosynê*, God's salvation, and of God's *dikaioun*, God's bestowing of his grace, he focuses attention entirely upon God. Everything is concentrated on the one vital question whether God is gracious or not, whether he grants his good pleasure or not, whether he says 'Yes' to me or 'No'. When does God say 'Yes'?

Paul answers: a man is justified, a man finds grace, through faith. Martin Luther, in his translation of Rom. 3.28, has added one word. He says: 'Therefore we conclude that a man is justified by faith only' ('allein durch den Glauben', *sola fide*). He has been criticized for this addition, but linguistically he was quite right. For it is a characteristic of the Semitic language (and, for that matter, Paul's epistles time and again betray his Jewish background) that the word 'only' or 'alone' is usually left out even in places where Western usage would consider it indispensable (cp. for example Mark 9.41: 'Whoever gives you a cup of water to drink because you bear the name of Christ, will by no means lose his reward,' where the sense is: 'Whoever gives you only a cup of water'; even this insignificant service will be rewarded). *Sola fide!* Faith is the only way to find God's grace.

When Paul speaks about finding grace by faith alone it is always in contrast to finding grace by works. The doctrine of justification cannot be understood without this antithesis. It is directed against the basic conception of Judaism and Judaizing Christianity, according to which man finds God's grace by the fulfilment of the divine will. Paul also held this view up to the moment when Christ appeared to him on the way to Damascus. But this moment ended for him the illusion that man can stand up before God on his own strength. And so, from Damascus on, he counters the thesis of the Judaists, that the observance of the law is the way to salvation, with the antithesis: the way to God's grace is not by deeds, rather it is by faith (Gal. 2.16; 3.8, 24; Rom. 3.28, 30; 4.5).

Thus faith replaces works. But then the question arises: Are we again confronted with some achievement on the strength of which God is gracious, if the justification follows because of faith? The answer here is: Yes! We are, in fact, confronted with an achievement. God does in fact grant his grace on the basis of an achievement. But now it is not my achievement, but the achievement of Christ on the cross. Faith is not an achievement in itself, rather it is the hand which grasps the work of Christ and holds it out to God. Faith says: Here is the achievement—Christ died for me on the cross (Gal. 2.20). This faith is the only way to obtain God's grace.

That God grants his good pleasure to the believer is against every rule of human law. This becomes clear, when one considers who is justified: the ungodly (Rom. 4.5), who deserves death because he bears the curse of God (Gal. 3.10). God's good pleasure is granted to him 'of grace' (Rom. 4.4; 5.17), as a free gift (Rom. 3.24). This grace knows of no restriction; being independent of the Mosaic law, it can also include the Gentiles. In Rom. 4.6–8 we have in a nutshell what is implied by this finding God's good pleasure *sola gratia*: 'David pronounces a blessing upon the man to whom God reckons righteousness apart from works:

> "*Blessed are those whose iniquities are forgiven, and whose sins are covered;*
> *blessed is the man against whom the Lord will not reckon his sin.*" '

Justification is forgiveness, nothing but forgiveness for Christ's sake.

Yet this statement needs further clarification.

2. *Justification and New Creation*

If we list the Pauline passages where the justification formula occurs, we come across an astonishing fact which is often overlooked, namely that the doctrine of justification is missing altogether in most of the Pauline Epistles. If we take the oldest of them, the two letters to the Thessalonians, we find no trace of it. In the first letter the adverb *dikaiôs* indicates the blameless behaviour of the

apostle (I Thess. 2.10). In the second, God's judgment is
called 'righteous judgment'; God is called 'just' because
his judgment is impartial (II Thess. 1.5f.). These statements have nothing to do with the doctrine of justification.
In Galatians, which is the next letter chronologically, the
full formula 'justification by faith' or 'to be justified by faith'
suddenly appears for the first time. In the two letters to the
Corinthians *dikaiosynê* has the meaning 'salvation', and 'to
be justified' occurs at least once (I Cor. 6.11) in the
specifically Pauline sense: but nowhere does the full
formula of 'justification by faith' appear in either letter.
We then find the full formula most frequently in Romans.
But again, it is missing in the Captivity Epistles,
Philippians, Ephesians, Colossians, Philemon, except in
Phil. 3.9, where *dikaiosynê* (salvation) by law is set over
against the *dikaiosynê* (salvation) of God by faith. The
Pastoral Epistles do not contain the full formula, though
Tit. 3.7 uses the following variation: 'justified by his grace'.
Thus the full formula 'justification by faith' or 'to be
justified by faith' is limited to the three epistles, Galatians,
Romans and Philippians (and in the last to one verse only),
to which may be added Tit. 3.7. This is a very striking
fact. How is it to be explained?

The answer is: the doctrine occurs exclusively where
Paul is engaged in debate with Judaism. Certainly W.
Wrede[1] was right when he concluded that the doctrine of
justification was a polemic doctrine, arising out of the
dispute with Judaism and its nomistic theology. But
Wrede went even further, and, from the limited occurrence

[1] W. Wrede, *Paulus*, Tübingen, 1904 (Eng. trs., *Paul*, London, 1907).

of the formula, concluded that the doctrine of justification
does not stand in the centre of Pauline theology. A.
Schweitzer[1] seconded him with the now famous formulation according to which the doctrine of justification is but
a 'subsidiary crater, which has formed within the rim of
the main crater' of Paul's mystical experience of life in
Christ. Is this a correct conclusion? I think not. Both
Wrede and Schweitzer are mistaken in their failure to ask
one question, namely: How is justification bestowed? How
does God accept the ungodly? In this matter we see things
more clearly today because we have learned in the last dec-
ades that it is in baptism that this bestowal takes place. This
follows, for example, from I Cor. 6.11, where the verb 'to
be justified' is surrounded by baptismal terms and
formulae: 'But you were washed, you were sanctified, you
were justified in the name of the Lord Jesus Christ and in
the Spirit of our God' (cp. further Gal. 3.24–27; Rom. 6.7;
Tit. 3.5–7). Paul does not stress explicitly the connection
between justification and baptism for the very simple
reason that in the justification formula the term 'by faith'
includes baptism by way of abbreviation, as R. Schnackenburg has convincingly shown.[2] The connection of justification with baptism is so obvious to Paul that he feels no
necessity to state in so many words that it is in baptism that
God saves him who believes in Jesus Christ.

Here we must remind ourselves that Paul speaks and

[1] A. Schweitzer, *Die Mystik des Apostels Paulus*, °Tübingen, 1930,
220 (Eng. trs., *The Mysticism of Paul the Apostle*, London, 1931, 225).
[2] R. Schnackenburg, *Das Heilsgeschehen bei der Taufe nach dem
Apostel Paulus* (Münchener Theologische Studien, I. Historische
Abteilung 1), München, 1950, 120.

writes as a missionary. In the missionary situation, for the Gentile or the Jew who believed in the good news and decided to join the Christian congregation, baptism was the decisive act by which he was included among those belonging to Jesus as their Lord. Therefore, Paul incessantly stresses the importance of baptism, and he uses a multitude of illustrations to show to the newly converted what this rite means to them. He tells them: 'When you are baptized you are washed; you are cleansed; you are sanctified; you are buried in the water and by this burial you get a share in Christ's death and resurrection; you are putting on Christ like a garment; you are incorporated into his body; you are adopted and you become sons of God; you are circumcised with the circumcision made without hands, that is, you are made members of God's people; in short, you are included in the kingdom.'

The formula 'justification by faith' is but one of these manifold illustrations. It is the description of God's grace in baptism using a figure taken originally from the judicial sphere: God's grace in baptism consists in his undeserved pardon. It is that formulation of the grace of baptism which Paul created in conflict with Judaism. Therefore it is not a 'subsidiary crater', but it occupies a place of equal importance with all the other descriptions of the grace of baptism, cp. again I Cor. 6.11: 'But you were washed, you were sanctified, you were justified in the name of the Lord Jesus Christ and in the Spirit of our God.'

This statement has a far-reaching consequence, namely that the doctrine of justification should not be isolated. On the contrary, it can only be understood in connection with all the other pronouncements about baptism. God's grace through baptism is so comprehensive that each of the many illustrations, images and comparisons which Paul uses expresses only one aspect of it. If he speaks of ablution, the stress is upon deliverance from the uncleanness of the old existence. If he uses the image of the putting on of Christ, borrowed from the language of mysticism, the emphasis is upon communion, even unity, with the risen Lord. The same intention, with the additional connotation of the unity of Christians with one another, is expressed by the image of incorporation into the body of Christ. If he uses the expression 'the circumcision of Christ' the point is inclusion in the new people of God. Finally, if he adopts the originally forensic language of justification, he intends to say that God alone is at work. Man does nothing; God does all.

Once again, no single image can exhaust the boundless wealth of God's grace. Rather, each is but a *pars pro toto* description which stands for the whole gift. Therefore, to isolate the forensic image could lead to a misunderstanding. It would lie in the conclusion that the grace of God given in baptism is merely forensic, that we are dealing with a mere 'as if': God acquits the ungodly and treats him as if he were righteous.

This came out very clearly in 1924 in an interesting controversy between R. Bultmann and H. Windisch, at a time when dialectic theology was enjoying its vogue. Bultmann wrote on 'The Problem of Ethics in Paul'.[1]

---

[1] 'Das Problem der Ethik bei Paulus', *Zeitschrift für die neutestamentliche Wissenschaft*, 23 (1924), 123–140.

His subject was the problem of the apparent contradiction between indicative and imperative, i.e. the paradoxical antinomy which we find for instance in I Cor. 5.7: 'Cleanse out the old leaven that you may be fresh dough, as you really are unleavened,' or in Gal. 5.25: 'If we live by the Spirit, let us also walk by the Spirit.' Bultmann rejected most emphatically and convincingly previous attempts at a merely psychological solution of this problem. In contrast, he stressed the eschatological character of divine justification. He insisted rightly that justification is not a change in the moral qualities of men, that it is not an experience akin to mystical experiences, that it can only be believed in. But I think he was misled when he added that the continuity of the old and the new man is not interrupted, that the believer does not cease to be ungodly and that he is always justified only as an ungodly person. Bultmann himself admitted freely that Paul does not say this. But he maintained that Paul had not pressed his thinking to its own conclusions and that the modern interpretation must make explicit what Paul omitted. Windisch contradicted Bultmann in the same year, 1924, in an article entitled 'The Problem of the Pauline Imperative'.[1] Windisch was an exponent of the old liberal school and several of his assertions clearly betray this. But he recognized the weak point in Bultmann's view. He remarked ironically that Paul evidently urgently needed to listen to a lecture by Karl Barth or perhaps Rudolf Bultmann (p. 278). Against Bultmann he insisted that

[1] 'Das Problem des paulinischen Imperativs', *ibid.*, 23 (1924), 265–281.

according to the apostle the continuity between the old and the new is completely broken, as radically as by death and resurrection ('If any one is in Christ, he is a new creation', II Cor. 5.17). Briefly stated, the *pneuma* is a reality which takes possession of the baptized and breaks the continuity between the old and the new existence.

This controversy is instructive in so far as the position of Bultmann (which, by the way, he did not maintain in his *Theology of the New Testament*) shows how dangerous it is to isolate the doctrine of justification. If we contend that the believer does not cease to be ungodly and if justification consists merely in a change of God's judgment, then we come dangerously near to the misunderstanding that justification is only an 'as if'. This surely was not Paul's intention. We have seen that for him justification was only one of the many attempts to describe the inexhaustible and unutterable riches of God's grace and that we must include justification in all the other sayings interpreting baptism in order to put it in its proper setting.

Now the common denominator of all sayings on baptism is that they describe God's gracious action as resulting in a new creation ('If any one is in Christ, he is a new creation'). And this new creation, Paul continues, has two sides: 'The old has passed away, behold, the new has come' (II Cor. 5.17). The old existence has come to an end; sin is washed away; the domination of the flesh and of the dark powers, including law, is broken. A new life begins: the gift of God's Spirit is granted and it manifests itself as an effective power. Whoever is incorporated in

Christ does not remain what he was. Christ is his life (Col. 3.4); Christ is his peace (Eph. 2.14). We always find these two aspects: God has delivered us from the power of darkness and has transferred us into the kingdom of his dear son (Col. 1.13).

This is also true of justification. Although it is quite certain that justification is and remains a forensic action, God's amnesty, nevertheless the forensic image is shattered. God's acquittal is not only forensic, it is not an 'as if', not a mere word, but it is God's word that works and creates life. God's word is always an effective word. The forgiveness, the good pleasure which God grants, is not only negative, i.e. an effacement of the past, but it is an ante-donation of God's final gift. (The word 'anticipation', which one might expect to be used here, is an unfortunate expression because it is derived from the Latin *anticipere* meaning 'to take in advance'. The sense at this point seems much better served by the word 'antedonation', which means a 'donation made in advance'.) As an ante-donation of God's final acquittal, justification is pardon in the fullest sense. It is the beginning of a new life, a new existence, a new creation through the gift of the Holy Spirit. As Luther put it: 'Where remission of sin is, there is life and salvation.'

The new life in Christ, given in baptism, is renewed again and again in the Eucharist. It is true that the verb 'to be justified' does not appear when Paul speaks about the Lord's Supper. But this is not astonishing, when one considers that Paul, by chance, deals with the Eucharist at length only in I Cor. 10 and 11, both of which are

concerned with practical questions, i.e. the sacrifice offered
to idols and the sharing of the meal with the poor brethren.
Both of these sections, especially I Cor. 10.16, show that
Paul understood the Eucharist to convey the same gift as
baptism: a sharing in Christ's vicarious death and in the
communion of his body. Thus, the Eucharist renews God's
grace given in baptism for which justification is but one of
many descriptions.

As an antedonation of God's final salvation, justification
points to the future. It shares the double nature of all gifts
of God: they are present possessions and yet objects of hope.
Justification is a firm present possession (Rom. 5.1, etc.)
and nevertheless it lies at the same time in the future, as
emphasized, for example, in Gal. 5.5: 'For through the
Spirit, by faith, we wait for the hope of salvation (*dikaiosynê*).' Justification, then, is the beginning of a movement
towards a goal, namely towards the hour of the definitive
justification, of the acquittal on the day of judgment, when
the full gift is realized.

For this reason, God's justification of the sinner is no
dead possession, rather it imposes an obligation. God's
gift can be lost. The justified still stands in the fear of God.
Justification takes place in the tension between possession
and hope. But it is hope grounded on a firm foundation.
In Rom. 5.8f. we read: 'God shows his love for us, in that
while we were yet sinners Christ died for us. Since, therefore, we are now justified by his blood, much more shall
we be saved by him from the wrath of God.' This is not a
conclusion *a minori ad maius* but *a maiori ad minus*: God has
done the greater thing: Christ died for us while we were

sinners—how much more, being justified, can we be certain that he will grant us the final salvation.

To sum up: it remains true that justification is forgiveness, nothing but forgiveness. But justification is forgiveness in the fullest sense. It is not only a mere covering up of the past. Rather, it is an antedonation of the full salvation; it is a new creation by God's Spirit; it is Christ taking possession of the life already now, already here.

3. The Origin of the Pauline Doctrine of Justification

Is Paul's doctrine of justification entirely new? Or does it have an older root? Is this doctrine that God gives his good pleasure to the ungodly because of his faith, purely by grace, to be found earlier than Paul?

It has recently been maintained that the Qumran texts anticipate what Paul had to say about justification.[1] Reference has been made primarily to the surprising similarity to Paul allegedly displayed by the concluding psalm in the Manual of Discipline (1QS 11.2ff.). It has been held that this passage attests the presence of the doctrine of justification *sola gratia* in Qumran. The text has been translated as follows:

> *But as for me, my justification* (mišpaṭi) *belongs to God,*
> *and in his hand is the blamelessness of my conduct,*

[1] S. Schulz, 'Zur Rechtfertigung aus Gnaden in Qumran und bei Paulus', *Zeitschrift für Theologie und Kirche* 56 (1959), 155–185; G. Klein, 'Rechtfertigung I', in *Die Religion in Geschichte und Gegenwart*[3], V, Tübingen, 1961, cols. 825–828.

together with the uprightness of my heart,
and in his righteousness my transgression will be wiped out
(1QS 11.2f.)
From the source of his righteousness comes my justification
(mišpaṭi),
a light in my heart from his marvellous mysteries (11.5).
If I stumble in sinful flesh,
my justification (mišpaṭi) *will remain eternally*
through God's righteousness (11.12).
Through his mercies he let me approach
and through his gracious manifestation comes my justification
(mišpaṭi);
by the justice of his truth he has justified me (šᵉphaṭani)
and in his great kindness he will atone for all my sins,
and by his justice he will cleanse me from all human uncleanness
(11.13f.).

Does this text warrant the conclusion that has been
drawn from it? The interpretation of the lines quoted above
hinges upon the word *mišpaṭ*, which has been rendered by
'justification' in the above translation. But this translation
is not correct. For neither in the Old Testament nor in the
literature of Late Judaism does *mišpaṭ* designate anywhere
the justification of the ungodly, nor does *šaphaṭ* mean to
justify the ungodly. The translation cited above, current
though it may be, does not accurately convey the intention of the text. Rather, careful attention to the words
which are used in parallelism with *mišpaṭ* shows that
mišpaṭ is God's gracious decision over the path of the life
of him who prays.[1] This decision is realized in God's

---

[1] I have my son Gert Jeremias to thank for pointing this out to
me. He further referred me to the almost literal parallel to 1QS
11.10f. that occurs in the Hymns Scroll 1QH 15.12f., where
instead of *mišpaṭ* we read: 'the inclination of every Spirit'.

letting the supplicant 'approach' (a technical term for entrance into the community) and thereby making possible for him the 'blameless conduct' in perfect obedience to the Torah, a conduct which man is not able to achieve by himself. If he stumbles on this path, God wipes out his sins and maintains his decision, provided the heart of the supplicant is sincere. Thus, *mišpaṭ* is not *justificatio impii*, the justification of the ungodly, but rather predestination to the path of perfect obedience to the Torah.

A particularly instructive example of how inadmissible it is to put Paul and Qumran on the same level is furnished by the interpretation the Habakkuk Commentary (1Qp Hab.) gives to Hab. 2.4, the central proof-text for the Pauline doctrine of justification: 'The righteous shall live by his faith.' 1QpHab. 8.1–3 reads: 'The interpretation (of this verse) concerns all the doers of the law in the house of Judah (and) those whom God will rescue from the house of judgment (that is, the Last Judgment) because of their labour and their loyalty towards the Teacher of Righteousness.'

Qumran says: God will save him who fulfils the law, faithfully following the Torah as interpreted by the Teacher. Paul interprets Hab. 2.4 quite differently: God grants life to the ungodly man who renounces all self-achievement and believes in Jesus Christ.

No! Qumran is not preliminary to Paul. Qumran is indeed aware of God's goodness and God's forgiveness, but they are valid only for those who attempt to fulfil the law to the last ounce of their strength. To sum up, Qumran and Paul belong to two different worlds: Qumran stands completely in the line of the law, Paul stands in the line of the good news.

But if Qumran does not represent a preliminary stage to the Pauline doctrine of justification, we do in fact find a prefiguration at one other point; we do find the teaching that the keeping of the law and pious achievements do not count with God, that he does not want to deal with the righteous but with the sinner. One other person before Paul said this: Jesus.

It is the message of Jesus concerning the God who wants to deal with sinners which Paul takes up and expounds in his doctrine of justification by faith. This message, unique and unprecedented, was the centre of Jesus' preaching. This is shown by all those parables in which God embraces those who are lost and reveals himself as the God of the poor and needy, as well as by Jesus' table-fellowship with the publicans and sinners. The fact that Paul takes up this message of Jesus is easily overshadowed, if one confines oneself to the concordance. It is true that many of the most important terms used by Paul, such as faith, grace, church, occur in only a few places in the sayings of Jesus. Nevertheless the substance of all these terms is present there. For example, Jesus usually does not say church (*ekklêsia*) but he speaks of the flock of God, the family of God, the vineyard of God. Paul constantly translates into theological vocabulary what Jesus had expressed in images and parables taken from everyday life.

This is also to the point regarding the doctrine of justification. The doctrine is nothing else but Jesus' message of the God who wants to deal with the sinners, expressed in theological terms. Jesus says: 'I came not to call the righteous, but the sinners'; Paul says: 'The ungodly man is justified.' Jesus says: 'Blessed be the poor'; Paul says: 'We are justified by grace.' Jesus says: 'Let the dead bury their dead' (a powerful word which implies that outside the kingdom one finds nothing but death); Paul says: 'He who is justified by faith will have life.' The vocabulary is different, but the content is the same.

According to Luke, Jesus occasionally used even the forensic terminology of justification to describe God's bestowing of his good pleasure upon the lost. We have quoted earlier Luke 18.14: 'It was this man, I tell you, who went home justified, and not the other,' and we have seen that the meaning is: 'It was this man, I tell you, who went home having found God's good pleasure, and not the other.' At this point Luke cannot be dependent on Paul on linguistic grounds for he uses a non-Greek idiomatic Semitism avoided by Paul.[1] We must conclude, then, that not only the content of the Pauline doctrine of justification but also the terminology of an antedonated eschatological pardon goes back to Jesus.

It was Paul's greatness that he understood the message of Jesus as no other New Testament writer did. He was the faithful interpreter of Jesus. This is especially true of his doctrine of justification. It is not of his own making but in its substance conveys the central message of Jesus, as it is condensed in the first beatitude: 'Blessed are you poor, for yours is the kingdom of God' (Luke 6.20).

[1] Cp. my book, *The Parables of Jesus*, revised edition, London and New York, 1963, 141f.

FOUR

The Revealing Word

1. The Literary Form of the Johannine Prologue

As THE beginning of a book, the Prologue of the Gospel of John is a unique passage. What the normal opening of a book was can be observed in the other five books which the New Testament contains, besides the twenty-one epistles. Here we find two forms employed. The first one is represented, for instance, by Rev. 1.1: 'The revelation of Jesus Christ, which God gave him to show to his servants what must soon take place; and he made it known by sending his angel to his servant John.' The opening passage here is a summary of the contents of the whole book. The preface to the Gospel of Luke is similar. In it we are told about preceding investigations, sources, and the intention and special character of the book. In the same way Luke prefaced the second volume of his work, the Acts of the Apostles, with a summary of his first volume. The other usual way of beginning a book is employed in Matt. 1.1: 'The genealogy of Jesus Christ, the son of David, the son of Abraham,' and, probably, in Mark 1.1 which could, or rather should, be translated: 'How Jesus Christ, the Son of God, began to announce the good news.' Here, in each case, the opening consists in the heading of the first chapter. In other words a book is ordinarily begun, either with a preface to the whole work or with the heading of its first chapter.

The Gospel of John is quite different, confronting us with the enigmatic opening: 'In the beginning was the Word.' In order to understand this peculiarity, we must direct our attention to the literary form of John 1.1–18. Three observations may be in order.

The first observation concerns sentence structure. The Prologue is constructed by means of parallelism, the pairing of similarly sounding clauses, constituting a kind of call and response—perhaps echoing the alternation between precentor and congregation. We are familiar with this literary form from the Psalms. In the Near East, parallelism has the same function as the use of rhyme in our languages: together with metre, it distinguishes poetry from prose. In other words, John 1.1–18 is a poetic passage. The Prologue, as everyone knows today, is a powerfully contrived song, an early Christian religious poem, a psalm, a hymn to the Logos Jesus Christ.

This Logos-hymn divides itself naturally into four strophes:

First strophe (vv. 1–5): The Logos of God;
Second strophe (vv. 6–8): The witness pointing to him;

Third strophe (vv. 9–13): The fate of the Logos in the world;

Fourth strophe (vv. 14–18): The confession of the believing community.

There are three forms of parallelism which are commonly used: the synonymous (the second line repeating the content of the first), the antithetic (the second line saying the opposite of the first) and the synthetic (the second line adding a new idea to the first).[1] But in the Johannine Prologue we find a very pronounced and seldom used fourth kind—a skilful elaboration of the synthetic form, namely climactic parallelism (step-parallelism). It is so named because every line takes up a word of the preceding line, as it were lifting it up a step higher. In the Synoptic Gospels we find an example of this form in Mark 9.37 (and par.):

> *Whoever receives one such child in my name*
> *receives me;*
> *and whoever receives me,*
> *receives not me but him who sent me.*

In the Johannine Prologue, it is represented, for instance, in 1.4f. and 1.14b, 16 (leaving out v. 15 for reasons which will be mentioned presently):

> In him was *life*,
> and the *life* was the *light* of men.
> And the *light* shines in the *darkness*,
> and the *darkness* has not comprehended it.

[1] C. F. Burney, *The Poetry of Our Lord*, Oxford, 1925.

> We have beheld his *glory*,
> *glory* as of the only son from the Father,
> *full* of *grace* and truth,
> and from his *fulness* have we all received *grace* upon *grace*.

This climactic parallelism is the dominating formal feature of the Prologue. It is, however, lacking in some verses. We observed already that in vv. 14–16 we could only obtain a climactic parallelism by the catchword 'full of grace' which connects v. 14b with v. 16, omitting v. 15. Similarly, vv. 12b and 13 also are devoid of climactic parallelism. This observation corresponds to another one. Whereas the climactic parts of the Prologue differ in their vocabulary from the Fourth Gospel (such important words as 'the Logos', 'grace and truth', even 'grace', do not recur outside the Prologue), the non-climactic insertions betray the language of the Fourth Evangelist himself (vv. 6–8, 12b–13, 15 and, perhaps, 17–18). It has, therefore, rightly been concluded and commonly accepted that we have to distinguish in the Johannine Prologue between the original Prologue (*Urprolog*, almost certainly composed in Greek) and the comments of the Evangelist about it. In the same manner we find quoted in Phil. 2.6–11 a pre-Pauline Christ-hymn, in which Paul has inserted comments. R. Bultmann maintained that the original Prologue came from the circle of the followers of John the Baptist, but this is refuted by Luke 1, which shows that the disciples of the Baptist spoke of the miraculous signs at his birth but did not ascribe pre-existence to their master. This means that the *Urprolog* must be of Christian origin. It was one of the hymns sung at the daily

74

Eucharist *Christo quasi Deo*, 'to Christ as to a God' (as Pliny puts it in his famous *Letter* X 96 to Trajan).

Now we can go a step further. The Logos-hymn is one of many in the New Testament. Like all mission churches and all vital communities, the early Church was a singing Church. The flow of new life, and the surging of great spiritual energy in the Church naturally made themselves felt again and again in song, hymn and praise. Psalms were on every lip. 'Let the word of Christ dwell in you richly, as you teach and admonish one another in all wisdom, and as you sing psalms and hymns and spiritual songs with thankfulness in your hearts to God' (Col. 3.16 par. Eph. 5.19). The services of the early Church were one continual jubilation, one great concord of worship and of praise.

In this rejoicing, in these hymns, we find a wealth of different themes. It is hardly by chance that we find the greatest number of hymns and doxologies in the Book of the Revelation. Here the dominating themes are the praise of God, the eternal king, and of the Lamb together with the thanksgiving for deliverance. The persecuted Church is always one step ahead, and amidst tribulation she anticipates in her hymns the final consummation. In the same manner the final salvation is anticipated in the two hymns in Luke 1, *Magnificat* and *Benedictus*. Rom. 11.33ff. extols God's inscrutable ways, I Cor. 13 praises love. Other psalms exalt Christ: Phil. 2.6–11; Col. 1.15–20; I Tim. 3.16; II Tim. 2.11–13.

Of all these New Testament hymns, the one undoubtedly most akin to the Christ-hymn in John 1 is Phil. 2.6–11. Not only are both songs about Christ, not only would

Pliny's phrase *Christo quasi Deo* apply to each of them (cp. Phil. 2.6 and John 1.1), but they also differ from all the other hymns in the New Testament[1] in that they relate, narrate and preach the story of Christ. They are *Heilsgeschichte in Hymnenform*. This literary genre, in which the history of salvation is chanted in psalmodic form, comes from the Old Testament; we need only compare the psalms extolling God's guidance of his people throughout their history, for example Ps. 78.[2]

Two examples from the second century AD, taken from different, even opposite realms, may show the development of this literary genre in the early Church and illustrate it at the same time. The first is the second article of the Creed, which tells and confesses in hymnic praise the story of Jesus Christ to the time of the parousia. The second example is the so-called Naassene Hymn, transmitted by Hippolytus in his book, *Refutation of all Heresies*. It begins by naming the three principles underlying all that exists, then gives a dramatic account of how the soul, like a timid deer, is hunted by death and is unable to find any escape from the labyrinth, and how Jesus offers to save it.

> *The world's producing law was Primal Mind,*
> *And next was First-born's outpoured Chaos;*
> *And third, the soul received its law of toil:*
> *Encircl'd, therefore, with an aqueous form,*
> *With care o'erpowered it succumbs to death.*

[1] Heb. 1.1–4 is very akin to them but does not show the pattern so distinctively.
[2] =Psalm 77 in the Greek and Latin Bible.

Now holding sway, it eyes the light,
And now it weeps on misery flung;
Now it mourns, now it thrills with joy;
Now it wails, now it hears its doom;
Now it hears its doom, now it dies,
And now it leaves us, never to return.
It, hapless straying, treads the maze of ills.
But Jesus said, Father, behold
A strife of ills across the earth
Wanders from thy breath [of wrath];
But bitter Chaos [man] seeks to shun,
And knows not how to pass it through.
Bearing seals I shall descend;
Through ages whole I'll sweep,
All mysteries I'll unravel,
And forms of Gods I'll show;
And secrets of the saintly path,
Styled 'Gnosis', I'll impart.[1]

What we have here is a Christ-hymn which begins, like the Johannine Prologue, with primordial origins and then tells about the pre-existent Christ and his compassion. Again we are confronted with *Heilsgeschichte in Hymnenform*. And yet, the Naassene Hymn on the one hand, Phil. 2, John 1 and the Creed on the other hand, belong to two entirely different worlds: Gnostic Christianity and the Gospel. To characterize these worlds bluntly: Gnosticism affirms that the greatest of all evils is death, but the Gospel affirms that the greatest of all evils is sin. Gnosticism asserts that the way of salvation is revealed knowledge (*gnôsis*), but the Gospel asserts that the way to salvation is pardon for our sins.

[1] Hippolytus, *Refutation of all Heresies* V 5, trs. J. H. Macmahon (Ante-Nicene Christian Library VI), Edinburgh, 1868, 153.

Nevertheless, we must take a final step. At one point in the hymn, there is a break, an interruption. The first three strophes (vv. 1–13) are cast in the third person. The last strophe (vv. 14–18), it is true, starts in the same way ('The Word became flesh') but immediately changes to the first person: 'We have beheld his glory, we have received grace upon grace.' That means that the Christ-hymn ends in a personal confession, it reaches its climax in thanks, praise and adoration. There can be no doubt, that it is not the opening part, the first three strophes, which contains the real substance of the psalm, but rather the confession of faith in the last strophe. Everything which comes before is only an introduction, a prelude, which serves to prepare for this confession. The Prologue is not primarily a dogmatic passage presenting us with Christological speculations about Christ's pre-existence, his part in the creation of the World and his incarnation—to take it so would be a grave misunderstanding. Rather is it the hymnal exaltation, by the believing community, of God's unspeakable gift through him in whom God's glory has been revealed.

Why did the Evangelist place this hymn to Christ at the beginning? Is it, as has been held, a summary of his Gospel? If so, the passion and the resurrection should have been explicitly mentioned. The right answer is to be drawn from the context. The story of John the Baptist follows in 1.19ff. This shows that the Prologue stands in the position which is occupied in Matthew and Luke by the birth- and infancy-narratives. The Fourth Evangelist has no account of the nativity, but rather replaces the Christmas story with the Logos psalm. The community of faith, so to speak, can no longer be satisfied with the prose-version of the incarnation—it falls on its knees and worships with a hymn of praise: 'We have seen it, we have experienced it, "we have beheld his glory".'

We now have the answer to our question, how the strange beginning of the Gospel of John is to be explained. The Evangelist begins his book on an exalted note. Apparently, he has the feeling that the pronouncement of the Gospel is incompatible with the usual sober pattern of the beginning of a book. Therefore, he starts with the powerful Logos-hymn, teaching us that the proclamation of the Gospel can never strike too high a note.

2. The Train of Thought

The first strophe (vv. 1–5)

Here the Logos is presented in a threefold manner.

'In the beginning was the Word.' The Logos-hymn starts with an intentional reminiscence of the first words of the Bible: 'In the beginning God created the heavens and the earth' (Gen. 1.1). But the word 'beginning' has a different meaning in the Prologue from what it has in Genesis. It does not designate the creation (which is mentioned only later, in John 1.3), but eternity before all creation. In other words: 'In the beginning' in John 1.1 is not a temporal concept, but a qualitative one, equivalent to the sphere of God. The Logos has its origin in eternity, those who deal with the Logos have to deal with the living God himself.

Then, the Logos is presented as the mediator in creation. 'All things were made through him, and without him was not anything made that was made.'[1] What is the meaning of this *theologoumenon*? Verse 10 gives the answer. 'He was in the world, and although the world was made by him, it did not recognize him.' That the world was made through him is the ground for the claim of Jesus Christ to sovereign authority over all. Thus, v. 3, 'all things were made by him', says: all men stand under the claim of the Logos —everyone, whether he acknowledges this or not.

Finally, this Logos was the light of men. 'In him was life, and the life was the light of men.' That the Logos was the light of men has often been misunderstood in that it was thought to mean that the Logos imparted the inner light—the light of reason and of insight—to all human beings. Clearly this is not the meaning. As the following sentence ('the darkness has not comprehended it') shows, this light is not of this world. Rather, this light is the light of the new creation, the eschatological light, with its strange double effect of making the blind see and the seeing blind (John 9.39). This saving light shone in the darkness, but it shone in vain—'the darkness has not comprehended it'. Men loved the darkness more than the light.

[1] Some scholars combine the last words with those that follow ('What was made, was life in him'). But this hardly makes sense. The creation 'was' not *zoê*, that is life in the fullest sense. Only the Logos 'was' life.

The second strophe (*vv. 6–8*)

Before the Evangelist continues his quotation of the hymn, he inserts a short passage of his own which tells how God announced the coming of the Logos through a prophet called John. The Baptist is honoured as the God-sent witness to Christ, but any overestimation of him is sharply repudiated. 'He was not the light' (v. 8). This statement must have been of great concern to the Evangelist because he stresses it again in v. 15, another of his insertions: the Baptist witnessed to Christ as being superior to himself because Christ came from eternity. The reason for this warning not to overestimate the Baptist may be found in the situation of the Church of Asia Minor at the end of the first century AD: Acts 19 suggests that there was a rivalry at Ephesus between the followers of the Baptist and the Church. But the reason could also be a personal one: perhaps the speaker here is someone who himself once had thought of the Baptist as the light until he met Jesus.

The third strophe (*vv. 9–13*)

Now the hymn goes on telling us more about the fate of the Logos in the world. 'The true light that "lights" every man was coming into the world' (v. 9). It is important to understand the clause 'that "lights" every man' correctly. It has often been interpreted to mean, 'which enlightens every human being'. But this Platonic understanding of the light as an inner light shared by all human beings is in contradiction to v. 5 (cp. p. 80) as well as to vv. 7f. 'To light' rather signifies 'to throw light upon, to reveal', and it is exactly in this way that John 1.9 is interpreted in 3.19–21. Thus, the sentence 'the true light that "lights" every man was coming into the world' says that the eschatological light which shone into the darkness had an all-revealing power. With an unavoidable clarity which could not be deceived it brought out the state of man before God. This revealing power of the Logos was the reason why the world 'knew him not' (v. 10), which does not mean that the world did not recognize him because he was disguised but rather (in an Old Testament usage of 'to know') that the world denied him, and refused to obey him. Even among 'his own', in Israel, he stood before closed doors, a stranger even on his own estate (v. 11). Such was the fate of the Logos in the world.

Yet not everywhere. There were some who received him; and where he was admitted, where men believed in him, there he brought a gift above all gifts—'to them he gave power to become children of God' (v. 12a). What it means 'to become a child of God' is explained by the Evangelist in an additional remark which makes use of a fundamental notion of Johannine theology: dualism. Again and again, the Fourth Gospel repeats that there are two kinds of life, two possibilities of existence: life from below and life from above, flesh and spirit, natural life and life through rebirth, earthly sonship and divine sonship.[1]

[1] It was rather tragic that the commentary on the Gospel of John by R. Bultmann (Göttingen, 1941), to which the author is deeply indebted, appeared six years before the Dead Sea Scrolls were found. For Bultmann founded his gnostic interpretation of the Fourth Gospel

This dualism is used in v. 13 to clarify the gift of the Logos, 'to become children of God'. Natural birth, though not to be despised in itself, does not enable man to see God as he is. There is only one way to God: rebirth, and there is only one who can give it: the Logos.

The fourth strophe (vv. 14–18)

The story of the Logos reaches its climax with the confession of the believing community. It begins: 'And the Word became flesh and dwelt among us' (v. 14a). In our days we can hardly imagine how scandalous, and even blasphemous, this sentence must have sounded to John's contemporaries. It contained two offences. The first is the word 'flesh'. 'Flesh' describes man in contrast to God by pointing to his frailty and mortality; it is the strongest expression of contempt for human existence. To say 'the eternal Logos became flesh' is to say that he appeared in profound abasement. Even more offensive must have been the words 'and dwelt among us'. For 'to dwell', 'to tabernacle' is a biblical metaphor for God's presence (cp. for example Rev. 7.15; 21.3; Mark 9.5; Luke 16.9). He 'dwelt among us' implies that God himself was present in the flesh, in abasement. Here the decisive question arises. How can one say this? How can one say of a man who felt

on the assumption that the Johannine dualism is of gnostic origin. But the Scrolls showed that the dualism of the Fourth Gospel has nothing to do with Gnosis but is, rather, Palestinian in origin; for like the dualism of Qumran it displays three decisive characteristics, each of which is non-gnostic: the Johannine as well as the Essene dualism is monotheistic, ethical and eschatological (expecting the victory of the light).

hunger and thirst, who knew fear and trembling, who died as a criminal—that God was present in him?

The answer is a simple confession consisting of two clauses. The first states: 'We have seen his glory.' The Greek text uses a verb here (*theasthai*) which has a special meaning. Like the usual word for 'to see' (*horan*) in the Fourth Gospel, it always denotes a real seeing with physical eyes, but, unlike *horan*, it can designate a seeing which penetrates beneath the surface. Thus 'we beheld his glory' says: We have seen the flesh, the lowliness of shame, the deep disgrace of the cross, but behind this veil of flesh and humiliation we beheld the glory of God. What does 'the glory of God' mean? The answer is given by the two-fold phrase 'full of grace and truth'. This is Old Testament covenant-language. 'Grace and truth' summarizes what the faithful experienced in the covenant: 'The Lord, the Lord, a God merciful and gracious, slow to anger, and abounding in grace and truth' (Ex. 34.6). 'I am not worthy of the least of all the mercies and of all the truth which thou hast shown to thy servant' (Gen. 32.10). In the covenant, the pious of the Old Testament had a double experience. They experienced God's mercy, of which they were unworthy, and more than this, God's truth, his constancy in this mercy. 'Grace and truth' describe the steadfastness of divine mercy. This was precisely the glory which became visible in Jesus. Those who belonged to him encountered in him the constancy of God's faithfulness. In everything that he did and said, one and the same thing always emerged, 'grace and truth', an unchanging divine mercy.

But the testimony of the community goes beyond the confession 'we have beheld his glory, full of grace and truth', to include this statement as well: 'And from his fulness have we all received grace upon grace' (v. 16). We have not only beheld his unchanging grace but we have received it. The expression 'grace upon grace' describes an endless progression and intensification. Out of an inexhaustible well we received one gift of God after another, each gift being greater than the preceding one. Such was the disciples' experience of Jesus. This is the whole answer of the believing community to the question: how can you say that in the man Jesus the eternal God dwelt among us? The answer is provided by pointing to his glory, the constancy of God's mercy and grace: we beheld it and we received it.

Here ends the story of the Logos, but not the Prologue. Rather, as a kind of summary, two antitheses are added which conclude the hymn by emphasizing the significance of the revelation in Christ. This revelation is first of all contrasted with that of the Old Testament. 'The law was given through Moses; grace and truth came through Jesus Christ' (v. 17). Once before God had given to men a great gift, his law, his holy will. But this was only the preparatory revelation. Now, in Jesus, God has really revealed himself and the fulness of his unchanging grace. Above the law stands grace.

The second and final antithesis goes even further. Most boldly, it contrasts the revelation in the Son not only with the Old Testament but with the whole human quest for God. 'No one has ever seen God; the only Son, who is in the

bosom of the Father, he has made him known' (v. 18).
God is invisible. Nobody has ever seen him, nobody is able
to see him. The man who looks at God must die, for God
is the Holy One, and we are defiled by sin. Only the
begotten Son has seen him. He has made him known. In
the Son, the invisible one became visible. 'He who has seen
me has seen the Father' (John 14.9). In this final clause in
v. 18, the absolute and universal claim of the Christian
faith (*die Absolutheit des Christentums*) is proclaimed.

3. The Meaning of the Designation of Jesus Christ as Logos

Having understood that the Prologue is a psalm and
having tried to follow its train of thought, we are now in
the position to approach our main problem: what is the
meaning of the designation of Jesus Christ as 'the Word'?
Of all the titles used for Christ in the New Testament, this
is the strangest one. We encounter it only in the Johannine
writings (John 1.1, 4; I John 1.1; Rev. 19.13). Several
questions arise.

With regard to the origin of this title, I can only make a
passing suggestion here. It has often been said, and I
myself held the view for a long time, that it originated in
Gnosticism. But an examination of the sources has shown,
to my surprise, that W. Bousset[1] was completely right

---

[1] W. Bousset, *Kyrios Christos*, 1913, second edition, Göttingen, 1921,
305.

when as much as fifty years ago he observed that the Logos-concept plays a very limited role in Gnosticism. Where it does appear in early Gnosticism—as for instance in the Valentinian school—it clearly is taken from John 1. Therefore, it is not in the field of Gnosticism that we have to seek the pre-history of the Logos-title, but in the world of Hellenistic Judaism, where the 'Word' was spoken of as the revelation of God. This fact, I believe, has been somewhat obscured in earlier investigations, because they started at an unfortunate point. They began with Philo. However, Philo's Logos-concept is but a *potpourri* of Old Testament, Platonic and Stoic ideas which can hardly be directly connected with the Prologue. But the concept of the personified Logos as a means of God's revelation is much older than Philo. We find it already in the Septuagint. In the powerful description of God's theophany in Hab. 3, it says in the Hebrew text that pestilence (*debher*) marched ahead of God (v. 5). Now 'pestilence' (*debher*) in unvocalized form is written exactly like 'word' (*dabhar*). So it was erroneously translated by *logos* (*dabhar*) in the Septuagint, where Hab. 3.5 reads: before God 'shall come *logos*'. The impact of this concept of the Word as God's precursor is to be seen in Wisd. 18.15f., where God's Logos is depicted as a stern warrior with a sharp sword leaping down from the royal throne in heaven. This reminds us at once of Rev. 19.11ff., where the coming Christ is described as the hero on the white horse with a sharp sword issuing from his mouth, and where he is called 'the Logos of God' (19.13). Thus, perhaps, the title 'the Word of God' was first used by the Christians as an attribute of the coming Lord. In a second stage the title seems to have been applied to the earthly Lord (I John 1.1ff.) and to the pre-existent Christ (John 1.1ff.; I John 1.1) as well. If this is correct, the Prologue would reflect an advanced stage of the use of the title by the Church.

But, for the present purpose, our attention is focused not upon the problems of origin and development, but rather upon a special and more limited question, namely: what did the title 'the Logos' mean for the Evangelist's contemporaries? This has been strikingly expressed by a man who, at the time when the Gospel of John was written, was probably bishop of Antioch in Syria. In AD 110, about twenty to thirty years after the composition of the Gospel of John, a persecution of the Christians broke out in Antioch. The bishop of the town was arrested and sentenced to be brought to Rome in order to be thrown to the wild beasts in the arena. As he travelled as a prisoner through Asia Minor, the local churches sent messengers to greet him on his way to death. Ignatius, as was his name, in turn sent letters for the churches back with them. These letters are powerful witnesses to the Christian faith. In them, Ignatius adjures the churches to hold fast to their faith, and entreats them urgently not to try to free him or to stop him from praising the crucified and risen Lord in the arena, even in the very face of the wild beasts. In the letter to the church of Magnesia, Ignatius speaks of Christ as the Word of God: 'Jesus Christ, who is the Word of God, which came forth out of silence' (*Magnesians* 8.2).

Ignatius starts with the presupposition that God was silent before he sent Jesus Christ. God's silence is a notion which originated in Judaism,[1] where it was linked with the exegesis of Gen. 1.3: 'And God said: let there be light.' What was there before God spoke, asked the rabbis, and their answer was: God's silence.[2] The silence which preceded God's revelation in the creation also preceded the revelation of his wrath against Pharaoh[3] and will again occur before the new creation.[4] In the Hellenistic world 'Silence' became a symbol of the highest deity. We even have a prayer to Silence. In the Great Parisian magical papyrus, the so-called Mithras Liturgy (fourth century AD), the mystic who, on his way to heaven, is threatened by hostile gods or star-powers is advised to put his finger on his mouth and to ask Silence for help by praying:

> *Silence, Silence, Silence,*
> *—symbol of the eternal, immortal God—*
> *take me under thy wings, Silence.*[5]

A moving prayer! God is silence. He is utterly removed and does not speak. He is a hidden God. To this inscrutable silence man can only lift his hands and cry: 'Take me under thy wings, Silence.'

It is in a world which knew of God's silence as a token of his inexpressible majesty[6] that the message of the Christ-

[1] B. Schaller, *Theologische Literaturzeitung* 87 (1962), col. 785.
[2] IV Ezra 6.39; Syr. Bar. 3.7; Pseudo-Philo, *Biblical Antiquities* 60.2.
[3] Wisd. 18.14.
[4] IV Ezra 7.30; Syr. Bar. 3.7; Rev. 8.1.
[5] 4.558ff. (ed. Preisendanz) = *Mithrasliturgie* 6.21 (ed. Dieterich).
[6] Ignatius, *Ephesians* 19.1; *Philadelphians* 1.1, cp. H. Chadwick, 'The Silence of Bishops in Ignatius', *Harvard Theological Review* 43 (1950), 169–172.

ian Church rings out: God is no longer silent—he speaks. It is true, he has already acted: he revealed his eternal power through the creation, he made known his holy will, he sent his messengers, the prophets. But in spite of all this, he remained full of mystery, incomprehensible, inscrutable, invisible, hidden behind the principalities and powers, behind tribulations and anxieties, behind a mask which was all that could be seen. Still, God has not always remained hidden. There is one point at which God took off the mask; once he spoke distinctly and clearly. This happened in Jesus of Nazareth; this happened, above all, on the cross.

This is how the joyful confession of the psalm in praise of Christ at the beginning of the Gospel of John must have sounded in the ears of those who heard it for the first time: God is no longer silent. God has spoken. Jesus of Nazareth is *the* Word—he is the Word with which God has broken his silence.

Indexes

Biblical References

Index

Index

Ancient and Modern Authors